Mouth-watering beverage recipes for every taste.

These secrets from the kitchen of two creative homemakers —personally tested and tasted—are guaranteed to please your friends and family. Completely non-alcoholic and many caffeine-free, these delicious beverage recipes are healthful and perfect for every occasion. Dozens of tasty ideas for simple socials and sumptuous receptions are provided — fruit punches, holiday beverages, party refreshments, vegetable drinks, and milk-base beverages, to name just a few. Also included in this resourceful recipe book are the "Beverage Guide for All Occasions" and the "Holiday Beverages Calendar." You'll love these delicious drinks — quick to fix, pretty to look at, and good to every last drop!

THE NON-ALCOHOLIC DRINK BOOK

DOLORES M. DUNAH

AND

H. JEAN GROUDLE

Power Books

FLEMING H. REVELL COMPANY

Old Tappan, New Jersey

IN HONOR OF *our dear friend, Blanche.*
Her thoughtfulness and consideration for
others was an inspiration to us.

Contents

A Good Idea Multiplies

The original concept for our beverage cookbook came to us one day while sharing a beverage recipe. We thought, "How good it would be if we could compile for our friends a booklet of our favorite beverage recipes to be given as a gift." Then, our thought expanded to the idea of writing a cookbook of unique and tasty beverages designed to meet the need of all homemakers who wish to have a ready supply of beverage recipes free from alcohol. That day marked the beginning of a continual thoughtful adventure in our kitchens. Our work consisted of testing, retesting, and changing these recipes many times to give you the select in quality and quantity. These beverages will enrich a variety of menus and are most appealing and colorfully appetizing. You will find a *Holiday Beverages' Calendar*, a *Beverage Guide for All Occasions*, and an Index which designates recipes by name and chief ingredient.

Before each chapter there are some *Helpful Hints* which are particularly useful for that section. Some of these aids are of a general nature which apply to many different types of recipes.

Among these are hints on crushing ice. (Use a towel-covered hammer to crush ice cubes placed in a heavy paper or plastic bag.) Unless the manufacturer of your blender recommends ice crushing, use this method rather than the blender.

Some ingredients are used repeatedly, such as superfine sugar and white corn syrup. They are specified because they dissolve better in cold drinks and more quickly in preparing syrups and hot drinks. The colorless quality of *white* corn syrup makes a more desirable drink when color appeal is required.

Recipes marked with an asterisk (*) are blender recipes. It is suggested that liquid always be added to the blender before chopped vegetables to prolong the life of the blender. When recipes call for added ingredients, remove feeder cap and add a little at a time while motor is running. If your blender has no feeder cap, turn motor off, add ingredients and then turn motor on again to continue beating.

Since many large-quantity recipes call for ice molds, it is suggested that the mold be made several days in advance and that it be made with ingredients from the recipe to avoid diluting the beverage.

Carbonated beverages should always be added at the very last minute to insure full carbonation.

As you prepare the recipes in this book you will undoubtedly find your own variations of ingredients, methods, and preparation, perhaps especially suited to your family and your kitchen.

Now our seedling of an idea which grew into this book has happily come to full bloom.

Dolores M. DuNah
H. Jean Groudle

1

CHOCOLATE BASE

Helpful Hints

Syrups

Fourteen Chocolate Drinks

International Recipes

Helpful Hints

Here are some *quick* and *easy* ways to prepare chocolate drinks!

Chocolate Milk   Stir 3–4 tablespoons chocolate syrup into glass of cold milk and mix thoroughly. A covered jar or blender may be used to blend really thoroughly!

Frosted Chocolate   Stir 3–4 tablespoons chocolate syrup into glass of cold milk and mix thoroughly. Add a scoop or two of chocolate, vanilla (or other desired flavor) ice cream. Top with a puff of whipped cream.

Hot Chocolate   Stir in 2–3 tablespoons of chocolate syrup into one cup hot milk. Mix well and serve in a pretty cup or mug.

Iced Chocolate   Mix cold milk with 3–4 tablespoons chocolate syrup, using shaker, mixer, or blender. Iced Chocolate is at its best served over crushed ice with a topping of whipped cream.

Ground Chocolate   You will find ground cooking chocolate comes already prepared in cans.

Real Cocoa   When recipe calls for cocoa, real cocoa is used, *not* imitation or instant.

Variations   To *1 cup* hot or cold chocolate drink, add one of the following:

    1 teaspoon almond flavoring
    1 teaspoon anise flavoring
    2 teaspoons cherry syrup (maraschino cherry juice is good)

12

2 teaspoons lemon flavoring
1 teaspoon lime flavoring
2 teaspoons mapleine flavoring
2 teaspoons orange flavoring
2 teaspoons peppermint flavoring
2 teaspoons raspberry flavoring
2 teaspoons strawberry flavoring

Syrup

Try one of these delicious chocolate syrups! They may be used for making hot or cold chocolate drinks. Also, you may spoon them over desserts such as puddings or ice cream. They will keep approximately 2–3 weeks in a covered jar in the refrigerator.

Quick-as-a-Wink Cocoa Syrup   This syrup is a good beginning cooking project for Mother's Little Helpers! Yield: 1½ cups.

1 cup superfine sugar
½ cup cocoa
1 cup cold water

Mix sugar and cocoa well. Then add water and stir to a smooth paste. Bring to a boil over low heat, stirring constantly. Continue to cook over low heat for 5 minutes, still stirring. (Be careful not to burn chocolate.) Cool; you may then cover and store in refrigerator 2–3 weeks.

Ground or Bar Chocolate Syrup   Yield: 2 cups.

1 cup ground cooking chocolate
   or
3 1-oz. bars unsweetened chocolate
½ cup superfine sugar
dash salt

1 cup water
½ cup corn syrup
1½ tsp. vanilla

Melt chocolate in stainless steel saucepan on lowest heat. Add all ingredients except vanilla. Heat to a boil, and boil gently for 10 minutes, stirring constantly. Now add vanilla. Cool and store in covered container in the refrigerator. It keeps 2–3 weeks.

* **Chocolate Crunch Chuckle** A top of perfection chocolate drink! Serves 8–10.

1⅔ cups chocolate syrup
2 tbl. superfine sugar
1 cup heavy cream
3 cups cold milk
1½ tsp. vanilla
1 28-oz. bottle chilled soda water

Garnish: whipped cream and nuts (grated fine).

Pour chocolate syrup, sugar, 1 cup heavy cream, milk, and vanilla into blender. Blend on high speed for 10–15 seconds. Divide mixture evenly into eight tall glasses filled with several ice cubes. Fill remainder of glass with soda water. Stir gently. Garnish each glass with a puff of whipped cream and sprinkle with finely grated nuts.

* **St. Moritz Shake** Very best of chocolate drinks! Serves 2.

6 tbl. chocolate syrup
1½ cups chilled milk (see below)
2 tsp. superfine sugar
½ cup vanilla ice cream

Garnish: whipped cream, grated unsweetened chocolate.

* *All blender recipes in this book are indicated with an asterisk.*

Put all ingredients in blender, cover and turn on high speed for 20 seconds. Pour into chilled tall glasses and serve immediately. Garnish with a puff of whipped cream sprinkled with grated unsweetened chocolate.

Note: *In place of chilled milk in recipe, you may substitute half milk and half undiluted evaporated milk, or thin cream.*

Puff the Magic Dragon   Big and little dragons love this magic flavor! Serves 4.

> ½ cup chocolate syrup
> 2 cups cold milk
> 1 pt. chocolate ice cream

Garnish: *chopped maraschino cherries, whipped cream.*

Put all ingredients in a small mixing bowl. Beat with rotary beater until smooth. Serve with puff of whipped cream mixed with a few pieces of chopped maraschino cherries.

Chocolate Peppermint Cow   Serves 4.

> 1 qt. milk, chilled
> ¾ cup chocolate syrup
> ½ tsp. peppermint extract
> 1 pt. chocolate ice cream
> (may substitute peppermint stick ice cream)

Garnish: *whipped cream, crushed peppermint candy, or 4 peppermint candy canes for stirrers.*

Put milk, chocolate syrup, and peppermint extract into a large mixing bowl. Beat with a rotary beater until blended well. Pour into glasses and top with ice cream. Garnish with a spoon of whipped cream mixed with a few pieces of crushed peppermint candy! The children will enjoy peppermint candy cane stirrers.

* **Coquilla Nut Compliment**   Serves 2.

> 1 cup coconut milk, chilled †
> ½ cup pineapple juice, chilled
> 1½ tsp. coconut extract
> ¼ cup chocolate syrup

Place all ingredients in blender and turn on high speed for 60 seconds. Pour into glasses which have been filled with ice. A real compliment whatever the occasion!

† Note: Coconut milk may be purchased in specialty food stores. Whole milk may be used as substitution for coconut milk. Coconut milk is mild in flavor and thicker than whole milk.

Unsweetened Bar Chocolate

Ski Jump Chocolate   After the slalom races and ski jumping are over, invite a few friends back to your cabin and offer them this winner! Serves 5.

> 1 tsp. cornstarch
> ⅛ tsp. salt
> ½ cup superfine sugar
>   *or*
> ⅓ cup corn syrup
> ½ cup boiling water
> 2 1-oz. bars unsweetened chocolate
> 1 qt. milk, scalded
> ⅛ tsp. ground nutmeg
> 1 tsp. vanilla
> 1 cup whipped cream (optional)

Garnish: marshmallows.

Mix cornstarch, salt, and sugar in a saucepan. Add a little of the boiling water at a time, stirring to make a smooth paste. Now add chocolate. Put over low heat and stir constantly until the chocolate melts. Add scalded milk, nutmeg, and vanilla. Beat with a rotary beater until hot and frothy. (Optional: fold in 1 cup whipped cream.) Serve at once topped with marshmallows.

Chocolate Eclair   Serves 5.

> 3 1-oz. bars unsweetened chocolate
> ¾ cup superfine sugar
> ½ tsp. cinnamon
> 5½ cups hot milk

Garnish: whipped cream.

Melt the chocolate squares in a double boiler. Add sugar, cinnamon, and hot milk. Continue cooking, and when very hot remove from double boiler and beat with egg beater until frothy. Serve with a puff of whipped cream.

* Marshmallow Madcap   This chocolate is so delicious you better make enough for thirds and fourths! Serves 3.

> 1⅔ cup milk
> 2 1-oz. bars unsweetened chocolate cut in small pieces
> ¼ teaspoon vanilla
> ⅓ cup superfine sugar

Garnish: marshmallows, maraschino cherries.

Place ⅔ cup of milk, chocolate, and vanilla into saucepan. Bring syrup to a boil and boil for 5 minutes. Put remaining milk, boiled syrup, and sugar into blender. Blend on medium speed for 20 seconds. Return to saucepan and heat until drink is very hot. Serve with a maraschino cherry and marshmallow on a toothpick.

Cocoa

Thick and Rich, Hot or Iced Cocoa   Serve in a variety of ways! (See suggested variations at the beginning of this chapter.) Add different flavorings. A real child pleaser. Serves 6.

> ½ cup cocoa
> ¼ cup superfine sugar
> ¼ tsp. salt
> 1½ cups boiling water
> 3 cups milk *and*
> 1 cup evaporated milk
>   *or*
> 4 cups half and half

Garnish: marshmallows for hot cocoa.

Melt cocoa, sugar, and salt in saucepan. Add boiling water and stir to a smooth paste. Put on medium heat stirring constantly until mixture boils gently for five more minutes. Slowly stir in milk in three equal portions, and heat thoroughly. Remove from heat. Beat 1 minute until frothy. Serve immediately. Top with marshmallow.

or

Iced cocoa may be enjoyed by simply chilling cocoa until icy cold and serving over ice cubes.

International Recipes

Cha-Cha-Cha Chocolate—Brazil   Serves 4.

> 2 1-oz. bars unsweetened chocolate
> 1 cup hot water
> ½ cup superfine sugar

3 cups milk
1 tbl. grated orange rind, either fresh or dried
½ tsp. almond extract

Garnish: 4 cinnamon sticks, approximately 3" long.

Melt chocolate and water together in the top of a double boiler. Then, stir sugar into melted mixture over direct heat. Simmer for 5 minutes, stirring constantly. Gradually add milk, orange rind, and almond extract. Heat thoroughly, until bubbles ring the edge of the pan. Strain, and beat with a rotary beater until frothy. Serve in cups or mugs with a cinnamon stick for stirring and an added bit of flavor!

Montmartre Chocolate Blend—France   Serves 12.

4 1-oz. bars unsweetened chocolate
¾ cup hot water
1 cup superfine sugar
½ tsp. salt
¾ cup medium whipping cream
about 3 qts. of milk

Garnish: whipped cream, sprinkle of mace.

Melt chocolate in hot water over low heat, stirring constantly. Add sugar and salt. Bring to a boil. Reduce heat and simmer 3 minutes while stirring continually. Cool mixture to room temperature. Whip cream in a small bowl and fold into chocolate blend. This may be now stored in a covered jar in the refrigerator until ready to serve. When serving, put 1–2 tablespoons into each cup. Fill with very hot milk and stir well. Top with a puff of whipped cream, sprinkled with mace.

Acapulco Chocolate—Mexico   Serves 5.

2 1-oz. bars unsweetened chocolate
½ cup hot water

¼ cup superfine sugar
½ tsp. cinnamon
⅛ tsp. salt
3 cups milk
1 cup light cream
1 egg, beaten
1 tsp. vanilla
½ cup orange juice

In the top of double boiler, put hot water and chocolate. Cook over boiling water, stirring constantly, until a smooth paste is formed. Now add sugar, cinnamon, salt, and then stir in milk, cream, and beaten egg. Cook for ½ hour while beating frequently with a rotary beater. Just before serving, stir in vanilla and orange juice. Pour into festive mugs and enjoy the rich flavor!

* Chihuahua Chocolate—Mexico   Serves 12.

3 egg whites, unbeaten
¾ cup cocoa
1 tsp. cinnamon
¾ cup superfine sugar
3 qts. cold milk

Put egg whites, cocoa, cinnamon, sugar, and 1 cup of the cold milk in blender and turn on high speed for 10 seconds. Pour remainder of the milk and blended mixture into large saucepan and cook over low heat until steaming hot. Do not boil. Serve at once!

Toreador Chocolate—Spain   Serves 4.

4 1-oz. bars unsweetened chocolate
4 cups milk
1 cup superfine sugar
1 tsp. vanilla

dash ground cloves
1 egg

Put chocolate and milk into the top part of a double boiler. Stir until melted, then beat with rotary beater over the boiling water for 3–4 minutes. Beat in sugar, vanilla, and ground cloves. Heat until steaming hot. Put egg in bowl and beat until frothy. Then add chocolate mixture and beat to a frothy consistency. Pour into carafe. Serve at once.

2

FRUIT BASE

Helpful Hints

Seventy-Two Cold and Hot
Fruit Drinks

Steaming Sips
or Frigid Plunges

Helpful Hints

Crushed Ice Put ice in heavy paper or plastic bag and pound with hammer wrapped in towel to prevent bag from ripping. Pound until ice is finely crushed. (If you use your blender for this purpose make sure the manufacturer recommends its use for ice crushing.)

Frosted Glasses Dip rim of glass about ¾ inch deep into water or lemon juice. Drain slightly and then dip into granulated or confectioners sugar. Place glass in freezer for a few minutes to harden sugar and to frost glass. Fill glass carefully to avoid wetting the frosted rim. V*oila!* Elegance in just a few minutes' extra time.

Imitation Fruit Flavors Welcome unexpected guests with a ready supply of these fruit flavors. Just add ice cold water and a little superfine sugar to taste. Then serve one of these (or mix 'em!):

Apricot, Banana, Coconut, Concord Grape, Ginger, Lemon, Lime, Orange, Peach, Peppermint, Pineapple, Raspberry, Rose, Spearmint, Strawberry, Tropical Fruit, Wild Cherry, etc.

Lemon or Lime Juice Substitute Bottled or canned lemon or lime juice may be substituted in all recipes (read directions on bottle or can for exact proportions). We find that the freshly squeezed juice is best, but in a pinch this substitution will do nicely.

Lemon, Lime or Orange Juice Abundant Yield Cover fruit with water in a saucepan. Boil for 10 minutes; cool slightly. Squeeze for juice. You will obtain more juice this way!

Party Time Ice Cubes Fill ice cube tray with water. Now add a small live flower to each partition, or some sliced maraschino cherries, nuts, leaves, or pieces of cut-up fruit. You can mix a few drops of food coloring of your choice to the water to color it before freezing. Ice cubes may be made with a portion of your fruit drink recipe; then they will not dilute the drink!

Hint for Blender Cover When recipe calls for added ingredients while motor is running, remove feeder cap and add little at a time. If your blender has no feeder cap, turn motor off, and add ingredients; then, turn motor on again to continue blending.

Apple

Apple Rally Roster Serves 6.

>   1 qt. apple juice, chilled
>   1 7-oz. bottle ginger ale, chilled

Garnish: Make 6 toothpick spears alternating:

>   6 green maraschino cherries
>   6 orange quarters
>   6 pineapple chunks
>   6 unpeeled apple cubes, soaked in lemon juice

Mix apple juice and ginger ale in cold pitcher. Pour into frosted glasses. (See Helpful Hints at beginning of this chapter.) Serve with colorful garnish of toothpick spears in each glass.

Hot Apple Touchdown The crowd will roar over this touchdown! Serves 4.

>   4 egg yolks
>   ¼ cup superfine sugar
>   4 cups hot apple juice

Garnish: touch of nutmeg.

Beat egg yolks and sugar in bowl until creamy yellow in color. Stir hot apple juice into this mixture and serve immediately in mugs. Top with a touch of nutmeg.

Tangy or Piquant Apple Juice For a tangy twist, add 1 tablespoon of lime juice to one cup apple juice. For a piquant flavor, sprinkle glass of apple juice with choice of cinnamon or nutmeg.

Apricot

Sizzling Apricot Enchantment Watch the kids gather round your open window to whiff this delight! Serves 4.

      1 16-oz. can apricot nectar
      ½ lemon, sliced thin
      4 in. stick cinnamon
      3 in. piece vanilla bean, or 1 tbl. vanilla extract
      ¼ tsp. almond extract

Combine all ingredients and bring to boiling point. Reduce heat and simmer gently for 5 minutes. Remove from heat, cover and allow to stand for 2 hours. Strain. Heat before serving.

* Apricot Tango   Serves 2.

      2 cups apricot juice
      ¼ cup fresh lemon juice
      2 ice cubes

Blend apricot juice and lemon juice on high speed for 10 seconds. Add ice cubes and blend 10 seconds more. Serve immediately.

Flipper Dipper   Serves 6.

      6 cups apricot nectar
      2 pts. orange sherbet

Pour apricot nectar into glasses, float scoops of orange sherbet on top. Delicious! So easy, too!

Banana

* Banana Bubbles   Serves 1.

> 1 cup chilled orange juice
> 1 mashed banana

Garnish: thin slice of orange.

Blend both ingredients on high speed for 20 seconds. Serve in well-chilled glass with a slice of orange as a garnish.

Blackberry

* Glorious Blackberry   Serves 4.

> 1 cup orange juice
> 1¾ cups blackberries and juice (canned)
> 1 cup water
> ¼ cup white corn syrup
> 1 large bottle ginger ale (28 oz.)

Put all ingredients except ginger ale into blender. Cover and blend on high speed until smooth, about 1 minute. Strain, chill thoroughly. When ready to serve, pour into tall glasses over crushed ice. Add ginger ale to fill glass and serve.

Cantaloupe

* Cantaloupe Dawn   This exceptional drink is perfect for a morning brunch, garnished with fresh mint. For an evening patio party it can be garnished with a small scoop of lime sherbet. Serves 6.

1 medium-sized ripe cantaloupe (2 cups diced cantaloupe)
2 tbl. fresh lime juice
1½ cups fresh orange juice
2 tbl. superfine sugar
¼ tsp. vanilla

Garnish: 6 orange cups, crushed ice, fresh mint (optional), lime sherbet (optional).

To prepare orange cups: *Cut off thick slice from top of 6 large oranges. Squeeze out the juice. Carefully spoon out the pulp and put aside. Serrate edges of orange cups. Set in refrigerator to chill. (Or for a firm orange cup that stays together better—freeze them.)*

To prepare drink: *Peel cantaloupe, cut open and scoop out seeds. Slice and dice in about one-inch pieces. Pour juices into blender, add cantaloupe, one cup at a time while blending on medium speed for 20 seconds until smooth. Repeat, using remaining ingredients. Blend another 15 seconds. Pour over crushed ice in orange cups. Serve with straws cut in half.*

Cherry

* **Unique Rose Nectar** Suggest you serve with an Indonesian cuisine. Serves 4.

4 red roses
2 cups water
1 cup superfine sugar
2 cups cherry juice
        or
1 14-oz. package frozen cherries
¼ tsp. almond flavoring

Remove petals from stems, wash and simmer slowly in the 2 cups water, stirring often until petals turn white. Add the sugar and cherry juice (or the whole package of frozen cherries) and simmer for 15 minutes. Cool. Put into blender on high speed. Remove, strain and add almond flavoring. Stir well and serve in chilled glasses.

Cherry Tulip Serves 8–10.

>1 lb. fresh sour cherries
>2 cups water
>4 cups superfine sugar
>1 28-oz. bottle soda water, chilled

Wash cherries. Put into saucepan with one cup of the water. Bring to a boil, reduce heat, and simmer for 20 minutes. Filter the liquid through cheesecloth, pressing the cherries gently until all the juice is removed; reserve juice. At the same time, simmer 4 cups sugar with one cup remaining water for 5 minutes. Add the cherry juice and simmer 15 minutes more. Remove from heat, cool and pour into clean jar to be stored in the refrigerator. When ready to serve, put 3–4 tablespoons of this fruit syrup into an iced glass, add soda water and 2–3 ice cubes. Stir well and serve. So refreshing and worth the extra work to make!

Cider

Pumpkin-Faced Folly The witches, goblins, ghosts, and spooks are out tonight! Serve them a steaming hot treat on Hallowe'en! Serves 4.

>4 cups sweet apple cider
>6 whole cloves
>2 in. piece vanilla bean
>3 in. stick cinnamon
>1 pt. orange sherbet

Garnish: thin slices of orange studded with cloves (leftover cloves from drink may be used). Insert cloves in orange slices to make replica of nose and mouth of pumpkin. To make eyes, use mara-schino cherry sliced in half, stuck on with clove.

or for a

Steaming Sip

Bring cider and spices to a boil in saucepan. Strain and serve piping hot in mugs. Float orange slices on top of each mug.

or for a

Frigid Plunge

Serve the above icy cold. Top with orange sherbet and pumpkin-faced orange slice pushed into sherbet.

Apple Harvest-Time   A luscious beginning for your Thanksgiving feast. Its mellow fragrance perfumes the air. Really a taste treat. Serves 10.

> 1 qt. sweet apple cider
> 2½ cups unsweetened pineapple juice
> ½ cup fresh mint leaves
> 1 28-oz. bottle ginger ale, unchilled

Place all ingredients, except ginger ale, in saucepan. Heat to a boil. Then, remove from heat and steep for 5 minutes. Sieve. Heat to sizzling hot. Add unchilled ginger ale and serve immediately in mugs.

Cranberry

Beach Boys' Delight   Serves 8.

> 4 cups cranberry juice
> 2½ cups fresh orange juice

½ cup fresh lemon juice
1 cup pineapple juice
½ cup crushed pineapple
1 cup water
½ cup superfine sugar
1 tsp. almond extract
cracked ice

for a

Steaming Sip

Mix all ingredients except ice in saucepan. Heat until piping hot. Serve.

or a

Frigid Plunge

Pour all ingredients except ice into a large pitcher and mix well. Fill each glass ¼ full with ice. Pour drink over ice and serve immediately. Delicious, delightful, desirable!

In the Pink   Serves 4.

1 cup cranberry juice, chilled
½ cup orange juice
1 cup vanilla ice cream

Garnish: orange, pink and white mints.

Blend all ingredients on high speed for 30 seconds until smooth. Serve in small glasses set on a plate with several colored mints.

Colorful Carousel   Serves 8.

2 cups cranberry juice
1 cup apricot nectar
3 tbl. fresh lemon juice
2 cups crushed ice

Combine all chilled juices in pitcher. Add crushed ice, stir gently, and serve. You may want to float orange and lemon slices on top to make a party carousel!

Delicacy Debut   Welcome in the New Year with this entree! Serves 10.

> 1 qt. cranberry juice
> 1 qt. grape juice
> 6 cloves
> 3 in. stick cinnamon
> ½ cup brown sugar

for a

Steaming Sip

Put all ingredients in saucepan. Heat slowly until sugar dissolves. Strain. Serve very hot in cups. Happy New Year!

or a

Frigid Plunge

Prepare as directed above. Chill until serving time. Pour over cracked ice.

Think-Cranberry-Lime-Link   Truly an exceptional drink! Serves 2.

> 1 cup cranberry juice, chilled
> 1 cup lime juice, chilled
> (use lime frozen concentrate,
> mixed with water per directions
> on can)
> sugar may be used to suit your taste

Combine juices and mix well. Try serving as a different breakfast juice.

Fig

* Tamarind Fig Fancy   Serves 2.

>   2 cups fig juice
>   1 tbl. lemon juice
>   ½ cup tamarind syrup
>   2 ice cubes

Garnish: twists of lemon.
Note: Tamarind syrup is available in gourmet or Oriental food stores.

Put *fig juice, lemon juice, and tamarind syrup into blender. Cover and blend on high speed for 5 seconds. While blender is still running, add the ice cubes or crushed ice and blend until smooth and frothy. Serve with a twist of lemon in a well-chilled glass. A gourmet's gulp!*

Grape

Celestial Grape Juice   Serves 10.

>   ½ cup superfine sugar
>   1 qt. water
>   2 tbl. grated orange rind
>   6 whole cloves
>   3 in. stick cinnamon
>   1 qt. grape juice
>   ¼ cup lemon juice

for a

Steaming Sip

Combine sugar, water, grated orange rind, cloves, and cinnamon stick in a saucepan. Bring to a boil and simmer gently for 10 minutes. Strain, add grape juice and lemon juice. Reheat and serve steaming hot in mugs for a chilly evening after the football game.

or a

Frigid Plunge

Chill in refrigerator 2–3 hours and serve on a summer evening after a baseball game.

Grape Juice Concentrate

Place several bunches of concord grapes in a saucepan. Cover with cold water to about 2 inches over level of grapes and bring to a boil. Reduce heat and simmer for twenty minutes. Put through a sieve and press firmly to remove all juice. To each cup of juice add ¼ cup of sugar. Place in a saucepan, bring to a boil and simmer 5 minutes. Refrigerate until ready to serve. Pour juice into containers ⅞ full and freeze. This grape juice is a joy to make and to serve! It is beautiful in color and savory in flavor.

Hammock Sipper   Serves 4.

> 2 cups grape juice
> 1 cup orange juice
> 2 egg whites, stiffly beaten
> 2 tbl. confectioners sugar
> sprinkle of salt

Combine fruit juices and chill well. Beat egg whites until frothy. Add sugar and salt. Beat until stiff peaks form. Fold egg whites carefully into fruit juice. Serve and sip on lazy summer afternoon.

Grapefruit

* Crystal Cloud   A citrus eggnog! Serves 4.

     4 eggs, separated
     4 cups chilled grapefruit juice
     ½ tsp. almond extract
     ¼ cup superfine sugar

Garnish: sprinkle of nutmeg.

Beat egg whites until stiff. Set aside. In blender, beat egg yolks on low speed for 5 seconds. Gradually add grapefruit juice while beating constantly. Add almond extract and sugar. Now add this mixture to egg whites, gently stirring. Pour into well-chilled glasses and sprinkle with nutmeg. The egg whites will float on top, looking like a billowy cloud!

Pink Surf   Take this drink along to the beach! Serves 10.

     1 cup superfine sugar
     1 cup water
     2 cups unsweetened grapefruit juice
     1 cup orange juice
     ½ cup grenadine syrup
     1 qt. chilled ginger ale

Garnish: thin slices of orange and maraschino cherries.

Simmer the sugar and water together for 10 minutes. Cool. Add grapefruit juice and orange juice and chill for 2–3 hours. At serving time, add the grenadine and ginger ale; stir lightly. Serve in tall thin glasses over ice cubes. Garnish with slices of orange and maraschino cherries on a toothpick, placed on top of the glass.

Hawaiian

Coconut Telegraphs   Say *Aloha* to your friends with any of these luscious tropical refreshments! Mix these juices in any desired proportions, chill thoroughly, and serve extra cold!

    guava nectar and passion fruit nectar
    guava nectar and orange juice
    papaya and orange juice
    papaya and pineapple juice
    passion fruit nectar and papaya nectar
    passion fruit nectar and limeade
    passion fruit nectar and orange juice

* **Merry Mahalo**   Your *aikanes* (friends) will *Mahalo* (thank you) for this drink! Serves 4.

        2 cups passion fruit nectar, chilled
        2 cups soda water, chilled

Blend ingredients on low speed for 5 seconds. Serve without delay over crushed ice.

* **Hilo Rhythm**   Under a coconut tree—just my guava nectar and me! Serves 1.

        1 cup guava nectar
        1 cup crushed ice
        1 tbl. superfine sugar

Blend all ingredients on high speed for about 5 seconds. Serve immediately!

Floating Island   Serves 4.

> 1 cup papaya juice
> 1 cup guava juice
> 1 cup pineapple juice
> 1 pt. lemon sherbet

Garnish: sprig of mint, pineapple spears.

Blend all juices and chill for 2–3 hours. When ready to serve, add one scoop of lemon sherbet for each drink. Place a sprig of mint and a pineapple spear on top of each glass.

* Monkey's Request   Big and little monkeys will chatter with delight over this dandy drink! Serves 2.

> 2 ripe bananas
> 2 cups coconut milk
> 1 egg
> 1 cup orange juice

Garnish: thin slices of orange.

Blend all ingredients on high speed for one minute. Serve in well-chilled glasses, garnished with thin slices of orange.

Plumeria Blossom   Serves 4.

> 3 cups unsweetened pineapple juice
> 1¼ cups fresh orange juice
> 1 cup non-fat dry milk powder
> 2 ripe bananas, cut in pieces
> ½ pt. pineapple sherbet

Put fruit juices, dry milk powder, and banana in blender. Cover and blend on high speed for 10 seconds. While motor is still running, add pineapple sherbet and blend for 10 seconds more. Pour into tall iced glasses. Yummy good!

Kumquat

* Keen Kumquat Ade   Do you have a beautiful bush just full of ripe kumquats and know not what to do with them? This mellow refreshment will answer your need in a luscious way! Serves 4.

> ½ cup superfine sugar
> ½ cup water (for sugar syrup)
> 1 cup kumquats, washed
> 3 cups water (for drink)

In saucepan, combine sugar and water. Bring to boil, simmer for 5 minutes, and cool. Place 3 cups water into blender; cover and turn on low speed. Add 1 cup of kumquats, a few at a time until all are partially ground up. Strain, add to syrup, chill.

Note: 2–3 tablespoons of kumquat pulp may be mixed with drink to provide added flavor if desired. Serve very cold. A great summer cooler!

Lemon

Blue Ribbon Lemonade Syrup.   Serves 6.

> 1 cup fresh lemon juice
> 1¾ cups superfine sugar
> 1¾ cups water
> pinch of salt
> rinds of two lemons

Combine fresh lemon juice, rind, sugar, water and salt in saucepan. Slowly heat until sugar is dissolved. Remove from heat and let stand until cool. Remove rinds and discard. Cool in refrigerator in covered jar until ready to use. Use ½ cup lemonade syrup to an

8-ounce glass, filling remainder with ice water. Lemonade is best when served with lemons squeezed the same day.

Note: To save preparation time you may prepare syrup several days in advance by omitting lemon juice and rind. Then, the day you plan to serve, add lemon juice and rind to the sugar syrup.

Rosy Lemonade

Using recipe for Blue Ribbon Lemonade, make a rosy lemonade by adding maraschino cherry juice for color and flavor. Garnish each glass with a maraschino cherry and a slice of lemon on a toothpick, or put a long-stemmed rose into the glass! After all—it is a rosy lemonade!

Dazzling Topaz   This refreshment is a real gem! Serves 6.

> 1 cup warm water
> 1 cup white corn syrup
> ½ cup fresh lemon juice
> ½ tsp. mint extract
> few drops yellow food coloring
> 1 28-oz. bottle ginger ale

Garnish: sprigs of lemon leaves.

Stir corn syrup and water together. Pour into a covered jar and store in refrigerator. In pitcher, place cooled syrup, juice, extract, and just enough food coloring to make a delicate yellow. Just before you serve, add chilled ginger ale. Pour into ice-filled glasses, stir gently and add a sprig of lemon leaves. Scrumptious!

* **Chiffonade**   This makes a real delicacy drink to serve on a hot summer day with a light luncheon! Serves 4.

> 4 eggs
> ¾ cup fresh lemon juice

¾ cup superfine sugar
1 cup fruit (pineapple, peaches or strawberries)
1 28-oz. bottle soda water, chilled

Combine the first four ingredients in blender, cover and blend on high speed for 30 seconds. Pour evenly into four glasses; add ice cubes to each glass and fill with soda water. Serve without delay after stirring gently.

Teeny Tiny Tots Thirst Tamer   Serve this with straws for little ones and watch the shiny bright faces smile up at you with joy! Serves 10–12 (depending on how teeny a thirst).

2 cups superfine sugar
2 cups water
1 cup lemon juice
½ cup orange juice
grated peel of 1 orange
grated peel of 1 lemon

Garnish: 8 maraschino cherries (cut in quarters); scoops of lemon, lime, orange, and raspberry sherbet (one pint of each flavor).

Simmer sugar and water for 10 minutes, cool. Add fruit juices and grated peel. Fill each glass ⅓ full with this mixture, add crushed ice and water to nearly fill glass to top. Put a few pieces of maraschino cherry in each glass along with two scoops of sherbet. Mix up flavors for a colorful party atmosphere!

Grandma's Original Cucumber Lemonade   This is undoubtedly one of the best lemonades you will ever taste plus it is pretty to look at too! Serves 8.

1⅔ cups superfine sugar
1½ qts. water
2 cups fresh lemon juice
¼ tsp. salt

rind of two 7-in. cucumbers, cut in lengthwise strips,
1 in. wide

*In saucepan combine sugar, water, and ⅔ cup of the lemon
juice. Heat and stir until sugar is dissolved. Continue to cook until
mixture comes to the boiling point and boil for 5 minutes. Chill
thoroughly. Add remaining lemon juice. Place ice cubes in pitcher.
Peel the cucumber in lengthwise strips 1 inch wide. Place lengthwise with the green side to the outside of pitcher. Add lemonade.
Chill for one hour so that the cucumber rind will flavor the
lemonade.*

Lime

"Love" Match Lemon-Lime   Very good thirst quencher for the
climax to a summer tennis match! Serves 2.

 ½ cup fresh lime juice
 2–3 drops mint extract
 ¼ cup superfine sugar
 2 cups cracked ice
 2 12-oz. bottles lemon soda

Garnish: 4 thin slices fresh lime, 4 thin slices fresh lemon.

*Mix lime juice, mint extract, and sugar well. Fill glasses ¾ full
with cracked ice. Add lime mixture. Fill glasses to top with lemon
soda and serve.*

Gleesome Glisk   A simple but extra delicious drink! Serves 3.

 1 6-oz. can frozen limeade concentrate, undiluted
 1 8-oz. can ginger ale, chilled
 few drops of green food coloring
 1 pt. of orange sherbet

Garnish: sprigs of mint.

Mix limeade concentrate and ginger ale in pitcher. Fill glasses with ice and pour liquid over them. A scoop of orange sherbet tops off a drink with eye appeal as well as an appetite pleaser!

Grass Green Limeade   Serves 6.

> ¾ cup superfine sugar
> 6 cups water
> 1 cup lime juice

Garnish: 6 cherries or 6 strawberries or 6 sprigs of mint.

Place sugar and water in saucepan. Heat to slow boil and simmer for 5 minutes. Refrigerate until cold. Just before serving squeeze limes, and add to cold syrup. Fill 6 glasses with ice cubes. Pour limeade over the cubes. You may want to serve a bowl of superfine sugar to your guests if they want to sweeten the drink to taste.

Note: To make a really green limeade, add a few drops of green food coloring to your beverage before serving. Stir well. Garnish with a cherry, strawberry or sprig of mint.

Grass Green Limeade Twist   Serves 6–8.

Prepare Grass Green Limeade as in above recipe. Add 3 cups unsweetened pineapple juice. Mix well. Serve with twist of lime on side of glass, or omit the twist of lime and top with a scoop of lime sherbet. It's scrumptious!

Loganberry

Loganberry Loo   Serves 4.

> 4 cups loganberry juice
> 1 cup orange juice
> 1 pt. orange sherbet

Garnish: diced fresh pears, mandarin orange slices.

Mix chilled fruit juices. Pour into glasses, float sherbet, serve with garnish of diced pears and orange slices on a toothpick.

Orange

Fresh Orange Juice When juice oranges are inexpensive and plentiful, serve plain orange juice for a refreshing and welcome beverage. Chill oranges and squeeze just before serving. You may prefer to squeeze oranges ahead of time; if so place juice in container, cover and refrigerate for no longer than a couple of hours for the finest flavor!

Garnishes for Fresh Orange Juice—Select one or more of the following for attractive serving: 1 large luscious strawberry, with hull on, 1 fresh pineapple cube, small seedless grapes, sprig of fresh mint.

Orange Duet Serves 6.

> 1 qt. orange juice
> few drops almond extract, to taste
> 6 scoops orange sherbet
>   (or 1 pt.)

Add a few drops almond extract to orange juice. Pour into chilled glasses and top with a scoop of orange sherbet. Serve with straws. This is a real flavor winner!

Forget-Me-Not A colorful drink that will be much appreciated on a sweltering day in August! Serves 6.

> 1 qt. orange juice
> 1 pt. raspberry sherbet
> 1 28-oz. bottle soda water

Freeze orange juice in ice cube trays until moderately solid. Then remove from trays and beat with electric mixer in bowl until slightly slushy. Divide frozen orange juice slush and raspberry sherbet evenly into 6 glasses alternating with a layer of orange slush and a layer of raspberry sherbet. Finish filling glasses with soda water, stirring gently to slightly mix flavors. Serve right away with a long-handled spoon. Ah, delightful!

Cool Recliner Put your feet up, sit back and enjoy the Cool Recliner after an especially busy summer day in the garden! Serves 4.

> 2 cups fresh orange juice
> ½ cup superfine sugar
> 6 mint sprigs
> ¼ cup lime juice
> 1½ cups soda water, chilled

Bring 1 cup orange juice to boil, add sugar and mint. Stir until sugar is dissolved. Cool and strain. Add remaining orange juice and lime juice. Refrigerate until just prior to serving, then add chilled soda water. Pour into ice-filled glasses and serve.

* Mint Mystery? Your friends will want to guess the ingredients in this delight! Serves 4.

> 3 oranges, seeded, peeled, and cut in pieces
> 1 cup fresh diced pineapple
> ½ cup water
> ½ cup superfine sugar
> ½ cup after-dinner mints
> 4 ice cubes

Put oranges, pineapple, water, sugar, and mints into blender. Cover and blend on high speed for 30 seconds. Add ice while blender is running, one cube at a time, until ice is finely crushed. A little more ice may be added if the consistency is thicker than desired.

* Peppermint Candy Chimney   Excellent flavor and kids from 2 to 102 love this idea! Serves 8.

> 1 12-oz. can frozen orange juice concentrate
> ½ cup lemon juice
> 10 peppermint hard candies
> ½ cup superfine sugar
> 1 egg white
> ¼ cup grenadine syrup
> 2 28-oz. bottles ginger ale, chilled

Garnish: 8 peppermint candy canes.

Blend all ingredients except ginger ale on high speed for 1–2 minutes. Divide evenly among 8 glasses. Fill with ginger ale. Stir gently to mix. Add a peppermint candy cane to each glass.

Lady Lark   Very colorful, bright and cheery for breakfast or brunch!   Serves 4.

> 4 cups orange juice, well chilled
> ¼ cup cranberry juice

Garnish: 6 party sticks strung with: frozen pineapple chunks, fresh strawberries, green maraschino cherries.

Mix juices well. Prepare party sticks with garnishes. Serve and enjoy the rainbow of color!

* Oscillating Orange   Serves 4.

> 2 cups orange juice
> 2 cups lemonade
> ¼ cup maraschino cherry juice
> 2 ice cubes

Blend all chilled ingredients on high speed for 20 seconds. Serve right away—pronto!

Peach

Peach and Blackberry Pinnacle   Perfect way to use blackberries in season. An unusual and superb flavor! Serves 4.

> 2 cups peach nectar
> ⅔ cup fresh lemon juice
> ½ cup superfine sugar
> 2½ cups cold water

Garnish: 1 cup drained, rinsed, fresh blackberries; cracked ice.

Combine peach nectar, lemon juice, sugar, and water in pitcher. Stir. Fill glasses ¼ full with cracked ice. Pour mixture over ice and gently stir ¼ cup blackberries into each glass. Serve with straws and long-handled spoons.

* **Peach Tree-eat**   Arouse the taste buds! Serves 4.

> 1 16-oz. can peach nectar, chilled
> 1 pt. lemon sherbet
> ½ tsp. peppermint extract

Variation: try substituting 1 pt. orange sherbet and ¼ tsp. almond extract.

Blend all ingredients for 1 minute on high speed and serve immediately.

* **Nectar Newcomer**   Is there a newcomer to your neighborhood? Welcome her to your home with this peachy treat! Serves 4.

> 4 cups peach nectar, chilled
> 1 cup miniature marshmallows
> ½ cup lemon juice

Garnish: 4 green maraschino cherries.

Blend *peach nectar, lemon juice, and marshmallows on high speed for 30 seconds. Serve with a green maraschino cherry as a garnish.*

* Fresh Peach Pace   Keep pace with the latest! Serves 3.

>   1 cup fresh peaches, peeled and cut up
>   *or*
>   1 cup peach nectar, chilled
>   ½ cup fresh lemon juice
>   ½ cup superfine sugar
>   2 egg whites
>   4 ice cubes

Garnish: thin slices lemon.

Blend all ingredients on high speed for 1 minute, adding ice cubes one at a time until all are finely crushed. Garnish with lemon slices. Serve.

Pear

* My Heart's Choice   Serves 4.

>   2 cups pear nectar
>   ¼ tsp. almond extract
>   1 pt. raspberry sherbet

Blend all ingredients for 1 minute on high speed and serve immediately in frosted glasses. (See Helpful Hints at the beginning of this chapter.)

Specialty Trio   Serves 2.

>   1 cup pear juice, chilled
>   1 cup peach juice, chilled
>   1 cup limeade, chilled

Garnish: thin slices of lime.

Mix all ingredients well and serve with a slice of lime on edge of glass!

Pineapple

* Fresh Pineapple Juice

All will enjoy fresh and flavorful pineapple juice you have made yourself. Peel a large pineapple and cut into cubes. Extract juice by putting pineapple into blender on high speed for 15 seconds. You will find there will be very little pulp. Strain the juice and serve iced with a garnish of fresh mint sprigs.

Pineapple Highlights   Have fun with pineapple juice. Serve in a variety of ways! Use equal parts or any desired proportions of the following:

Pineapple juice and ginger ale
Pineapple juice and orange juice
Pineapple juice and loganberry juice
Pineapple juice and boysenberry juice
Pineapple juice and apricot juice with ice

Chill all ingredients and serve over cracked ice with garnishes of strawberries in season; slices of lime, orange, and lemon; red and green maraschino cherries.

* St. Patrick's Limelight
All the leprechauns will come running when the St. Patrick's Limelight is announced! Serves 4.

     1½ cups pineapple juice
     ¼ cup lime juice
     1 tsp. lime rind, finely grated
     1 ripe banana
     3 green maraschino cherries
     1 pt. vanilla ice cream
     few drops green food coloring

Blend all ingredients on high speed for 20 seconds until mixture is smooth. Pineapple and lime is a very good combination!

Exotic Pineapple   This is a good way to use leftover pineapple peelings! Listen to calypso music and enjoy an exotic pineapple. Serves 4.

> peelings from 1 medium pineapple
> peelings from 1 large orange
> 2 tsp. powdered ginger
> 1 cup superfine sugar
> 4 cups boiling water
> 1 cup fresh orange juice
> ¼ cup fresh lemon juice

Rinse pineapple and orange peelings, then place in a container with ginger, sugar, and boiling water. Cover and let stand overnight in refrigerator. Strain, add orange and lemon juice. Serve over cracked ice in well-chilled glasses.

Pomegranate

Positively Pomegranate   Epicurean tastes will appreciate this unusual beverage! Serves 4.

> 8 large pomegranates (about 2 cups juice)
> ½ cup lemon juice
> 1 cup superfine sugar
> 2 cups soda water, chilled

After cutting pomegranates into halves, squeeze out juice on a reamer exactly as you would an orange or lemon. Strain, add lemon juice and sugar. Stir well and chill. Serve diluted with soda water over cracked ice in frosted glasses. (See Helpful Hints at the beginning of this chapter.)

Prune

Attune of Prune   Serves 6.

> 6 cups cold prune juice
> ½ cup superfine sugar
> ½ cup lemon juice
> 1 pt. lemon sherbet

Mix prune and lemon juice with sugar. Pour into chilled glasses over scoop of lemon sherbet.

Prune Wrinkle   This is a new wrinkle! Watch for a pleasure twinkle! Serves 4.

> 2 cups chilled prune juice
> 2 cups chilled pineapple juice
> ½ cup superfine sugar

Garnish: 4 pineapple chunks, 4 whole prunes.

Combine juices and sugar. Stir well and serve immediately in well-chilled glasses. Garnish with a chunk of pineapple and a prune on a toothpick.

Pruneberry Attention-Getter   Serves 2.

> 1 cup prune juice
> 2 cups cranberry juice
> ¼ cup superfine sugar
> 2 scoops cranberry sherbet

Mix juices and sugar and chill thoroughly before serving. Float a scoop of cranberry sherbet on top of this delicacy.

Raspberry

Rainbow Cheer   A tantalizing flavor that is sure to excite pleasure! Serves 2 (large glasses).

>   20 oz. finely crushed ice
>   ¼ cup orange juice
>   ¼ cup raspberry juice
>   ¼ cup lime juice

Garnish: 2 maraschino cherries.

Fill two 10-ounce glasses with ice. To each glass add alternately half of each of the fruit juices. Pour juices slowly for a delightful rainbow of layered color. Garnish each glass with a maraschino cherry and serve with straws.

Switcheroo   Welcome refresher. Both of these drinks are delightful combinations! Serves 1.

>   1 bottle raspberry soda, chilled
>   2 scoops vanilla ice cream

Pour raspberry soda into tall glass. Add ice cream. Serve with straw and long-handled spoon.

or

>   1 bottle ginger ale, chilled
>   2 scoops raspberry sherbet

Pour ginger ale into tall glass. Top with raspberry sherbet and serve with straw and long-handled spoon.

Rhubarb

Strawberry-Rhubarb Jamboree   Sure to be a taste-pleaser for that crowd of scouts after their jamboree! Serves 6.

> 1 lb. fresh rhubarb
> (water for cooking)
> 1 cup fresh strawberries
> 1¼ cups superfine sugar
> ½ cup fresh lemon juice
> 1 cup water

Garnish: whole fresh strawberries.

Wash rhubarb and cut into 1-inch pieces. Place in saucepan. Add just enough water to cover rhubarb. Put a lid on saucepan and simmer for 15 minutes until rhubarb is tender. Strain, saving juice. (Pulp may be used for a dessert.) Add sugar to rhubarb juice and stir until dissolved. Refrigerate until cool. Crush strawberries with potato masher and strain through sieve. Put crushed strawberries aside to use later. Combine all juices and water. Pour crushed mixture into glasses filled with ice. A spoonful of crushed strawberries may now be scooped into each glass. Top with whole strawberry.

Spice

Snappy Ginger Syrup   Serve with Indonesian food! Both white and brown sugar syrups have excellent flavor. Try both to determine which you enjoy best. Serves 10.

> 10 slices ginger root
> 2 cups water

2 cups white sugar
or
1½ cups brown sugar

Garnish: thin slices lemon.

To prepare ginger root: *Use 1½ inch long piece of ginger root approximately 1½ inches in diameter. Wash, peel, and cut into ⅛ inch slices.*

Put ginger root, sugar, and water in a pan, cover, simmer for 20 minutes. Strain and cool. Pour into a covered bottle and store in refrigerator until ready to use. Just before serving, add 2–3 table-spoons syrup and half a glass of ice water. Stir well and fill remainder of glass with cracked ice. Garnish with thin slices of lemon on sides of glass.

Hot-Mulled Ginger-Fruit Smiles of approval will adorn your home when this scrumptious aroma floats through! Using the Snappy Ginger Syrup recipe make this drink with these added ingredients. Serves 4.

2 cups of Snappy Ginger Syrup
1 in. piece stick cinnamon
4 whole cloves
1⅓ cups orange juice
⅔ cup lemon juice

Put ginger syrup, cinnamon stick and cloves in saucepan. Cover and simmer for 20 minutes on low heat. Remove from heat. Add orange and lemon juices. Mix well and heat until piping hot. Serve immediately.

Strawberry

Strawberry Dewdrops   A delicious, delectable and de-lovely drink!
Serves 10–12.

> 2 pts. hulled fresh strawberries
> 2 cups superfine sugar
> ice water *or* crushed ice

Garnish: whole strawberries, hulls off, and dipped in water then into powdered sugar.

Put strawberries into a large bowl and cover with sugar. Mash with a fork or potato masher. Let stand in refrigerator for two days, occasionally stirring. Strain mixture and pour into a clean container. Serve diluted with ice water or undiluted over crushed ice. Use about ½ cup of strawberry mixture to ½ cup ice water or ½ cup crushed ice. Garnish with frosted strawberries on top.

Strawberry Ice Evermore   You get two-in-one with this drink specialty. A delicious drink and a dessert with whole or diced fruit. Serves 4.

> 1 cup lime juice
>   *or*
> 1 cup orange juice
> 1 cup unsweetened strawberry juice
> ½ cup superfine sugar
> 2 glasses crushed ice

Garnish: whole strawberries, melon balls.

Fill glasses ¾ full with crushed ice. Stir lime juice, strawberry juice, and sugar together well. Evenly divide this mixture into each glass. Garnish with whole strawberries and melon balls on a toothpick.

Tangerine

Gay Nineties   Serves 4.

> 1 egg white
> 1 tsp. grated lemon rind
> 4 cups tangerine juice
> 2 tsp. lemon juice
> 1 cup crushed ice

Garnish: 4 sprigs of mint.

Beat the egg white until stiff. Stir in lemon rind, tangerine juice, and lemon juice. Beat vigorously. Add the crushed ice and pour into a shaker. Shake well and serve, garnished with a sprig of fresh mint.

Tangerine Blossomtime   Out of this world! A real taste treat for a ladies' luncheon! Serves 8.

> 4 6-oz. cans frozen tangerine concentrate
> 6 juice cans ice water
> 2 envelopes unflavored gelatin
> 1 cup superfine sugar

Garnish: mandarin orange slices, green maraschino cherries, honeydew melon balls.

Mix tangerine juice with 3 juice cans of water. Pour ½ cup of this mixture into a small pan; sprinkle gelatin on top. Let stand for 5 minutes. Put pan on low heat and stir until gelatin is dissolved.

Add this along with sugar to remaining tangerine juice. Pour into refrigerator trays and freeze until mushy, about ½ hour. Remove from trays. Put into a chilled bowl and beat with rotary beater until fluffy. Garnish with a slice of mandarin orange, a green maraschino cherry and a honeydew melon ball on a toothpick.

3

FRUIT PUNCH BASE

Helpful Hints

Forty-Four Fruit Punch Drinks

Extra Special Hot Punches

Helpful Hints

To Prepare Ice Mold   Pour 1 inch of water into mold. Freeze. When frozen, remove from freezer and arrange fruit or other garnishes over frozen water. Add 1 inch more of water and refreeze. Then, fill mold to top with water and refreeze. To remove mold, dip into hot water and gently slide into already filled punch bowl. Note: Mold prepared with distilled water gives less cloudy appearance.

For Ease in Preparation   Make your ice mold 1–2 days in advance of serving punch.

Non-Diluting Ice Mold   A reminder! Make ice mold from your punch recipe. There will be no diluting of the punch when it melts.

Studded Garnishes   The lemon, orange, and lime garnishes for ice mold may be studded with such spices as cloves or whole allspice.

Variation and Pretty Effects   Obtain a variation and pretty effect with ice cubes by using these suggested garnishes in them: small flowers, maraschino cherries, nuts, fruits, or leaves; or a few drops of food coloring may be added to water before freezing.

Make a Spice Bag   Cut a square of cheesecloth large enough for your spices, insert spices and tie with string.

Tip for Carbonated Beverage   Reminder! This is a must: add ginger ale or carbonated water to punch at the very last minute; otherwise, you will have a loss of carbonated gas and might just as well use plain water.

Fast and Efficient Service Fill punch cups in kitchen. Serve on trays. Encourage serve-yourself refills.

A Touch of Grenadine Flavor and a pretty pink color may be given to any punch by adding 1 tablespoon or more of grenadine to punch.

No Punch Bowl? If you do not have a punch bowl use a large salad bowl or lively mixing bowl with ladle and paper cups. For hot punches, stainless steel mixing bowls or brightly colored dutch ovens make nice serving containers. Silver punch bowls are also available and are truly elegant.

Leftover Punch You may freeze leftover punch in ice cube trays and use in fruit juice, first removing fruit slices, if any. If freezing in plastic jars fill only ¾ full to allow space for expansion. Important Note: Due to flavor loss which sometimes occurs with freezing we suggest you freeze *only* leftover fruit punch drinks.

Apple

Delightful Discovery Yield: 20 punch cups.

> 1 qt. apple juice
> ½ cup lemon juice
> 1 cup orange juice
> 1 can crushed pineapple (13½ ounces)
> 1 28-oz. bottle ginger ale, chilled

Garnish for ice ring mold: ½ cup pineapple tidbits, 4 oz. maraschino cherries.

Combine fruit juices with pineapple and chill at least 3–4 hours. Just before serving pour juices into punch bowl and add ginger ale. Stir gently. Add ice ring mold and serve.

Apricot

Cascade Reception Punch   Happy Wedding Day! This punch has a tang and is pleasingly tart. Good accompaniment for a wedding cake! Yield: 24 punch cups.

> 1 12-oz. can frozen pineapple juice concentrate (unsweetened)
> 1 6-oz. can frozen grapefruit juice
> 1 6-oz. can orange juice
> 1 qt. ice water
> 1 12-oz. can apricot nectar, chilled
> 1 qt. ginger ale

Garnish: maraschino cherry ice cubes. (See directions in Helpful Hints in beginning of chapter.)

Open cans of frozen fruit juices and mix with the ice water. Stir until frozen juices dissolve completely. Add chilled apricot nectar. Stir to blend. When ready to serve, add ginger ale. Stir gently. Pour over ice cubes in a punch bowl. Put a maraschino cherry ice cube in each punch cup when serving.

Blackberry

Merry-Go-Round   This punch is easy to make and extra good, too—for your class reunion! Yield: 18 punch cups.

> 1 cup thawed frozen raspberries
> 1 cup raspberry juice
> 2 cups blackberry juice
> block of ice

    1 quart sparkling water
    1 quart lemon soda

Note: *sieve berries for more juice.*

Mix the thawed raspberries and juices. Cover and refrigerate until well chilled. Place block of ice, fruit, and juices in punch bowl and pour in well-chilled sparkling water and lemon soda. Serve directly in 4-ounce punch cups. (You can enjoy this luscious punch any time of the year by using canned fruit.)

Cherry

Mt. Vernon Punch   Why not serve this on Washington's Birthday? Yield: 45 punch cups.

    2 pkgs. sweetened cherry-flavored summer drink powder
    1 6-oz. can frozen lemonade concentrate
    1 6-oz. can frozen orange juice
    1 6-oz. can frozen pineapple juice
    3 qts. ice water
    ¼ cup grenadine syrup
    3 28-oz. bottles ginger ale, chilled

Garnish for ice mold: small bottle of maraschino cherries, 6 drops of red food coloring. (Prepare a day ahead according to directions in Helpful Hints.)

Combine all ingredients except ginger ale; mix well until frozen juices are thawed. Pour over cherry ice mold in punch bowl. Just before serving, add ginger ale and stir gently. Serve immediately.

* **Cherry Blossom**   So quick and easy to prepare. Guests are delighted with this beverage! Yield: 45 punch cups.

    3 cups cold water
    1 pkg. cherry-flavored summer drink powder (sugar added)
    10 ice cubes

Put cold water and drink powder in blender. Turn on low speed; add ice cubes one at a time until ice is crushed and serve.

Cider

Happy Holiday Punch   Make in 5 minutes for a crowd! Yield: 30 punch cups.

> 2 qts. sweet cider
> 3 cups apricot juice
> 1½ cups fresh orange juice
> ¾ cup fresh lemon juice
> 1 28-oz. bottle soda water, chilled

Garnish: 8 green maraschino cherries, quartered; 8 red maraschino cherries, quartered; 3 trays of ice cubes.

Chill all ingredients in advance of preparation. Combine all juices and mix well. Pour into punch bowl over ice cubes. Place the quartered red and green cherries in small dish beside punch bowl. When serving, spoon a few cherries in cup before pouring punch.

Cheepy Charley   Try a Cheepy Charley for a picnic. Mix on the spot! Yield: 50 punch cups.

> 1 qt. apple cider, chilled
> 18 oz. sweetened grapefruit juice, chilled
> 18 oz. orange juice, chilled
> 4 qts. ice water
> 2 pkgs. sweetened orange-flavored summer drink powder
> few drops orange food coloring

Mix all ingredients in large container and serve.

Pilgrim Punch   You don't have to be a turkey to gobble up this punch! Yield: 32 punch cups.

1 gallon sweet cider
½ cup superfine sugar
6 in. stick cinnamon
1 tbl. mace
1 tbl. whole cloves
1 tbl. allspice
1 tsp. salt
2 tbl. crystallized ginger, sliced
then
1 cup unsweetened grapefruit juice
½ cup orange juice
¼ cup lemon juice

Bring all ingredients except citrus juices to a boil. Lower heat and simmer for 10 minutes. Strain into a large pan. Cool to luke-warm. Then stir in citrus juices. Heat and serve immediately in punch cups.

Cheeri-up Cider   The last *Cheeri-up* of the robin as he flies **South** for the winter is an invitation to prepare this mulled cider punch. The appealing aroma waves good-bye to the robin and welcomes in the brisk autumn weather. Yield: 12 punch cups.

6 in. stick cinnamon
1 tbl. whole cloves
12 pieces of lemon or orange peel
2 qts. of sweet apple cider
½ cup brown sugar, packed
⅛ tsp. salt
¼ cup molasses, if desired

Garnish: small squares of orange or lemon peel.

Tie cinnamon, sugar, cloves, and peel loosely in spice bag. (See directions for spice bag in Helpful Hints at beginning of chapter.) Pour cider into a very large pan; add tied spices and molasses.

Bring to a boil and simmer for 5 minutes. Remove from heat and let cool 1 hour leaving tied spices in cider. Then, remove spice bag and refrigerate cider until just before serving. Serve sizzling hot with a piece of lemon or orange peel in each punch cup.

Cranberry

Santa's North Pole Punch As Santa Claus scoots down your chimney be there waiting to greet him royally with this delectable mellow aroma and beautiful hue. Yield: 20 punch cups.

> 1 tsp. whole cloves
> 1 6-in. stick cinnamon
> 1 tsp. coriander seed
> ½ cup unblanched almonds
> 1 cup raisins
> peelings of 2 oranges
> 1 qt. water
> 2 1-qt. bottles cranberry juice
> 3 cups pineapple juice
> 3 cups grapefruit juice

First, tie cloves, cinnamon, and coriander seed in spice bag. (See directions in Helpful Hints at beginning of chapter for making spice bag.) Place tied spices, almonds, raisins, peelings and water in saucepan. Simmer uncovered for 15 minutes. Add juices and reheat to serve piping hot. An almond and a few raisins may be spooned into each cup so that the pleasing flavor will linger to the bottom of the cup.

Cupid's Cupful A real lovey drink for your favorite Valentine! The cranberry flavor is definite and the beautiful red color is most appealing. Yield: 30 punch cups.

> 1 cup red currant syrup, or jelly
> 16 oz. cranberry juice
> ½ cup lemon juice
> ½ cup orange juice
> 3 28-oz. bottles ginger ale

Mix syrup, sugar and juices in container. Cover and refrigerate for several hours. Before serving stir well and add ginger ale. Serve over ice in punch bowl.

Swing Set Punch This combination of fruit juices will be declared delectable by all the swingin' set whether they are 6, 16, or 60. Yield: 36 punch cups.

> 1 pt. cranberry juice
> 1 qt. apple juice
> 12 oz. frozen lemonade concentrate
> 6 oz. frozen pineapple concentrate
> 6 oz. frozen grapefruit concentrate
> small block of ice or ice cubes
> 2 28-oz. bottles lemon soda

Garnish: lemon slices.

Chill all ingredients well in advance of serving time. Pour juices over block of ice in punch bowl. Mix well. Add carbonated water. Stir gently. Float slices of lemon in punch bowl or if served from pitcher garnish side of glass with a lemon slice.

Grape

(NOTE: *See directions under fruit base for making fresh grape juice!*)

Spicy Splash Don't splash a drop of this. It is too good to waste! Yield: 24 punch cups.

½ cup fresh mint leaves
10 whole cloves
1½ cups boiling water
1 6-oz. can frozen lemonade concentrate
1 6-oz. can frozen orange juice concentrate
2 6-oz. cans frozen grape juice concentrate
2 qts. cold water
large block of ice

Garnish: 2 oranges, sliced very thin.

Place mint leaves and cloves in a large pan. Cover with boiling water, let steep for 20 minutes. Strain. Now add the undiluted fruit juice concentrates and the cold water. Stir until blended. Pour the punch over a large block of ice in a punch bowl. Float orange slices, studded with cloves on top. Very festive!

Tokay Treasure   Superb punch for large crowds—very colorful, full-flavored, too! Yield: 130 punch cups.

4 cups superfine sugar
2 cups water
6 qts. grape juice, chilled
1 qt. lemon juice or orange juice, chilled
9 qts. ginger ale, chilled
large block of ice to float in punch bowl

Boil sugar and water for 10 minutes, to make a syrup. Cool in refrigerator about ½ hour. Mix syrup with grape and lemon juice. Just before serving, add ginger ale. Gently place a large chunk of ice in the punch bowl and serve.

Lavender and Old Lace Punch   This luscious punch is rich in grape flavor with just the right amount of lime. Many grateful smiles will thank you for this refreshment. Yield: 25 punch cups.

2 cups water
6 in. cinnamon stick

¼ tsp. whole cloves
4 cans frozen grape juice, undiluted
½ cup lime juice
2 qts. chilled ginger ale
Block of ice

Garnish: seedless grapes.

Combine water, cinnamon stick, and cloves in saucepan and bring to boil. Remove from heat and cool. Then chill for several hours. Strain spices from liquid. Combine with the grape and lime juices; mix well. Pour over the block of ice in punch bowl. Add ginger ale just before serving. For a special treat you may garnish with seedless grapes.

Grapefruit

* **Tangy Pacesetter** A real good conversational drink that is pleasingly refreshing. Yield: 6 punch cups.

1 cup superfine sugar
1 cup water
3 cups unsweetened grapefruit juice
1½ cups pineapple juice
1 cup lime juice

Garnish: mint sprigs. For rims: 3 tbl. powdered sugar, 2 tbl. lemon juice.

Combine sugar and water in saucepan. Bring to a boil and simmer for 5 minutes. Cool thoroughly. You may combine juices and water syrup in your blender on medium-high speed for 10 seconds. Then, refrigerate mixture until icy cold. (See directions at beginning of Fruit Base Chapter in Helpful Hints for frosting glass rims.) Pour chilled drink carefully into frosted glasses to avoid melting frosted rims. Sprigs of mint may garnish top of each glass.

Nestled Easter Bunny Punch   Make individual nests of green grass paper with colored candy eggs to give your table that certain flair at Easter time. Serve guests this drink they will never forget—a glorious regal gold color. Yield: 32 punch cups.

> 6 cups sweetened grapefruit juice
> 6 cups sweetened orange juice
> ½ cup fresh lemon juice
> 1 qt. ginger ale
> few drops of yellow food coloring
> 1 qt. of lemon sherbet
> 1 cup flaked coconut

Combine chilled fruit juices. Refrigerate. Using a small scoop, take balls of sherbet and roll in flaked coconut. Place on large shallow pan in freezer. At serving time pour juices into punch bowl. Add ginger ale and stir gently. Add small balls of sherbet. Serve and enjoy immediately.

Pops-a-Zesty Punch   A great treat for Pops on Father's Day—a tart flavor he will enjoy. Yield: 20 punch cups.

> 1 tbl. dried mint leaves
> 1 cup superfine sugar
> 1 cup water
> 3 cups pineapple juice
> 3 cups grapefruit juice
> 2 cups apricot juice
> ½ cup fresh lemon juice

Garnish for ice ring mold: 4 pineapple spears, 4 red and 4 green maraschino cherries, rinsed well; 4 lemon slices, about ¼ inch thick; few lemon leaves. (Prepare well in advance.)

Mix mint, sugar, and water in a small saucepan. Bring to a boil and simmer for 10 minutes. Strain out mint leaves; cool. Combine with juices. Chill. (See directions for preparing ice mold in Help-

ful Hints at beginning of chapter.) Pour juices into punch bowl and gently slide ice mold into punch and serve.

Hawaiian

Melanesian Island Punch   This is an extra good punch. Yield: 25 punch cups.

> 1 46-oz. can pineapple juice
> 1 12-oz. can guava nectar
> 1 12-oz. can papaya nectar
> 1 pt. lime sherbet (orange may be substituted)
> 1 qt. ginger ale

Garnish: 1 mango, sliced (optional).

Refrigerate juices until icy cold. Remove juice from cans and pour over sherbet in a punch bowl. Let melt slightly. Add ginger ale. If desired, float small slices of mango on the top and serve.

* Joy Poi Punch   Hawaiians love poi but many visitors do not at first taste. After using poi in this delightful punch, you will love it too! Yield: 8 punch cups.

> ¾ cup prepared poi
> 1 cup vanilla ice cream
> ⅓ cup superfine sugar
> ¼ cup maraschino cherry juice
> 2 cups milk

Garnish: dash of nutmeg, few maraschino cherries, cut up.

Blend poi, ice cream, sugar and cherry juice on low speed until smooth. Add milk gradually while blending. (See directions in

Helpful Hints for blender cover in chapter 2.) Sprinkle nutmeg and maraschino cherries over the surface of each serving.

* **Papaya Plush** Really want to treat your husband, family or guests? Serve this best-ever drink! Yield: 30 punch cups.

> 4 cups ripe papaya pulp (about 6 large ripe papayas)
> ¾ cup superfine sugar
> 1 cup cold water
> 1 12-oz. can passion fruit juice
> ¼ cup lime juice
> 2 12-oz. cans guava juice
> 2 cups orange juice
> 4 cups unsweetened pineapple juice
> ¼ cup grenadine syrup

Garnish: sprigs of mint, maraschino cherries.

Blend papaya pulp, sugar, and water in electric blender for 2 minutes on medium speed. Place in large bowl. Add remaining ingredients. Mix well and chill. Serve in small cups. Garnish with a sprig of mint and maraschino cherry. Makes a colorful thirst quencher!

Hawaiian Paradise An easy way to make punch that is delightful! Yield: 20 punch cups.

> 1 6-oz. can frozen pineapple juice, thawed
> 1 6-oz. can frozen orange juice, thawed
> 1 qt. of milk, chilled
> 1 qt. water, chilled
> 1 pt. sherbet (lime)

In large punch bowl, stir thawed pineapple and orange juices together with milk and water. Float scoops of lime sherbet on top of punch and serve.

Lemon

* **Lemonade Punch Base** Make-ahead work-saver for children's party. Yield: 8 glasses.

> 2 lemons, quartered and seeded
> rind of 1 lemon
> 1 cup superfine sugar
> 2 cups milk
> ½ tsp. lemon extract
> 2 28-oz. bottles lemon-lime soda

Place lemons, rind, and sugar in blender. Cover and start motor on low speed for 10 seconds. Turn on high speed and continue beating 1 minute until sugar is dissolved and rind is finely grated. Add milk and lemon extract. Blend another 1 minute on high speed. Chill. (This basic punch mix will keep 1–2 weeks in refrigerator in covered jar.) When ready to serve, place ice cubes in a tall glass. Add 2–3 tablespoons of the lemon mixture. Fill glasses with lemon-lime soda and serve.

Festive Poinsettia Punch Although the decorations of this drink are festive and delightful the scene-stealer is the wonderful flavor. Yield: 24 punch cups.

> 4 cups red currant juice concentrate, chilled
> 2 28-oz. bottles lemon soda, chilled

Garnish for ice ring mold: artificial poinsettias frozen in mold.

Following directions given in Helpful Hints at beginning of chapter, make an ice mold using a large mold. Freeze artificial poinsettias in mold instead of fruit. Pour currant juice and lemon soda into chilled punch bowl. Gently slide ice ring mold into

*punch. Live poinsettias may be placed around outside base of
punch bowl for holiday decoration.*

Lime

* Golden Mirth Punch　A perfect refreshment for a ladies' luncheon. Adorn your table with a yellow linen cloth and individual
bouquets of baby breath, tiny roses and maidenhair fern. You
might place fern around base of punch bowl and lay yellow tea
roses on top. Yield: 20 punch cups.

> 1 6-oz. can frozen lemonade concentrate
> 1 6-oz. can frozen limeade concentrate
> 1 6-oz. can frozen orange juice concentrate
> 2 qts. ice water
> 6 oz. limeade concentrate for ice ring

*(Prepare ice mold a day ahead using one 6-ounce can frozen
limeade concentrate mixed with enough water to fill mold.) Blend
fruit juices with water on low speed dividing portions and blending according to size of blender. Pour into punch bowl, gently add
ice mold and serve.*

Killarney Cooler　Enjoy on St. Patrick's Day. Also a real cool summer drink! Yield: 16 punch cups.

> 1 6-oz. can frozen limeade concentrate
> 1 4-oz. bottle green maraschino cherries plus juice
> 4 cans cold water
> 1 lime, thinly sliced

*Combine limeade, water and green maraschino cherry juice. Stir
until frozen concentrate is thawed. When ready to serve add ginger ale. Stir gently. Float thinly sliced lime in punch. Cut maraschino cherries in half and place in center of lime slices and serve.*

Orange

Hot Sunburst Punch   A cloudy day may be as bright as a burst of sunlight when you serve your guests or early morning sleepy-heads this cheering and flavorful hot drink. Definitely one of the best hot drinks you have ever tasted! Yield: 16 mugs.

>   2 qts. orange juice, fresh
>   1 cup superfine sugar
>   3 sticks cinnamon (6 in. each)
>   4 tsp. whole cloves
>   4 tsp. grated orange peel (or dehydrated orange peel)

Garnish: few orange slices, cut ¼ inch thick. (Grate orange before squeezing juice.)

Place all ingredients in saucepan. Heat to full boil for 1 minute, stirring occasionally to mix. Reduce heat and simmer for 3 minutes. Strain and discard spices from boiled mixture. Pour into heated metal punch bowl (see Helpful Hints for this chapter), or directly into mugs. You may float orange slices in punch or place one slice in individual mugs.

California Poppy   Goooo——d! Everyone will enjoy this excellent drink. Yield: 24 punch cups.

>   1 cup superfine sugar
>   4 cups water
>   1 cup fresh lemon juice
>   6 cups fresh orange juice
>   1 cup fresh raspberry juice

Garnish: lemon and orange slices. For ice mold: few drops of red food coloring, ¼ cup raspberries.

Note: To make fresh raspberry juice, crush berries and press through a fine sieve until you have 1 cup of juice (about a pint of berries should do it).

(See *directions for preparing ice mold in Helpful Hints at the beginning of chapter.) Refrigerate all juices for 3–4 hours prior to preparing. Mix sugar with 2 cups of the water and ¼ cup of the lemon juice. While stirring, bring to a boil. Reduce heat and simmer 1 minute. Add remaining water and refrigerate for ½ hour. Stir in chilled fruit juices. Pour into a punch bowl over ice mold. Float few slices of lemon and orange on top.*

Shanghai Special   Serving oriental food? Try this for a party a la oriental. Yield: 10 punch cups.

> ½ cup lemon juice
> ½ tsp. ground ginger
> 2 in. stick cinnamon
> 4 whole cloves
> ½ cup superfine sugar
> 4 drops peppermint flavoring
> 1 cup water
> 3 cups orange juice
> 1 cup grape juice
> 4 drops red food coloring

Slice lemons in ¼ inch slices; then, cut in quarters. Put in a large bowl along with ground ginger, stick cinnamon, whole cloves, sugar, peppermint flavoring, and water. Cover and chill for 3–4 hours. Strain and add chilled orange juice, grape juice, and red food coloring. Mix well. Serve in punch cups as a delightful appetizer for an oriental dinner.

Magic Carpet Float   What a punch for Mother's Day! Surprise her—this is really easy to make and ultra good too! Yield: 32 punch cups.

2 qts. orange, lemon or raspberry sherbet
2 qts. ginger ale, chilled

Put sherbet of your choice into punch bowl and add ginger ale at serving time. Mix with large spoon until sherbet is partially melted and serve.

Pineapple

Marigold Day Punch   The day your lovely marigolds burst into full bloom invite the Garden Club over for a luncheon. Serve this luscious punch with a ring of marigolds around the base of the punch bowl. Yield: 32 punch cups.

2 28-oz. cans pineapple juice, chilled
2 12-oz. cans apricot nectar, chilled
2 6-oz. cans frozen orange juice concentrate
2 6-oz. cans frozen lemonade concentrate
2 qts. ice water

Garnish for ice mold: few drops yellow food coloring, yellow and orange dwarf marigolds.

(See directions for preparing ice mold in Helpful Hints at beginning of chapter.) Combine all juices with water in punch bowl. Stir until frozen concentrates are dissolved. Place ice mold gently into punch and serve.

Labor Day Promenade   This is easier than pie for a Labor Day strut! Yield: 18 punch cups.

5 cups pineapple juice
4 cups grape juice
¼ cup fresh lemon juice

Mix all the juices together. Chill and serve. Excellent flavor!

Magna Cum Laude Punch   Yield: 36 punch cups.

> ¾ cup superfine sugar
> ½ cup lemon juice, fresh
> 3 qts. unsweetened pineapple juice
> 16 oz. cranberry juice
> 2 28-oz. bottles lemon-lime soda
> 1 qt. raspberry sherbet

Chill all liquids well in advance of preparing punch. Add sugar to lemon juice and stir until dissolved. Pour sugar and lemon juice into chilled punch bowl. Next, blend in remaining juices and carbonated beverage. Place scoops of sherbet into punch bowl stirring gently to partially dissolve and serve.

Surfer's Curl   After a hard day of battling the "big ones" the group will gulp gallons of this punch! Serve with hamburgers and potato chips. Yield: 45 punch cups.

> 1½ cups superfine sugar
> 1 cup water
> 4 cups orange juice
> 2 cups lemon juice
> 1 46-oz. can unsweetened pineapple juice
> 1 pt. strawberries, sliced in half
> ½ cup crushed mint leaves
> 3 28-oz. bottles ginger ale

Garnish: thin slices of orange peel. For ice mold: use half pineapple juice and half water. (See directions in Helpful Hints at beginning of chapter.)

Bring sugar and water to a boil in saucepan. Reduce heat and simmer for 10 minutes. Cool for ½ hour. Combine orange and lemon juices, strawberries, and crushed mint leaves. Pour into punch bowl or large serving container. Add ginger ale and stir gently. Float ice mold on top and serve.

Goldilocks' Chit-Chat Punch   A great hit for a fashion show or ladies' luncheon. Yield: 12 punch cups.

> 1 qt. chilled unsweetened pineapple juice
> 1 pt. orange sherbet
> 1 pt. vanilla ice cream
> 2 cups ginger ale

Garnish: thin slices of lemon.

Put juice, sherbet, and ice cream in large bowl. Blend well with electric mixer or egg beater. Pour into chilled punch bowl then gently stir in ginger ale, just before serving. Float thin slices of lemon in punch.

Raspberry

Wedding Ring Punch   Takes awhile to prepare for your special someone but this drink is definitely worth it. The ultimate! Yield: 32 punch cups.

> 3 3-oz. packages raspberry flavor gelatin
> 4 cups boiling water
> 1½ cups superfine sugar
> 5 cups ice water
> ½ cup lime juice
> 3 cups orange juice
> 1 cup lemon juice
> 1 28-oz. bottle soda water
> 2 10-oz. packages frozen raspberries, partially thawed
> 2 sliced bananas

Chill all ingredients for 3–4 hours. Dissolve gelatin in boiling water. Then add sugar, cold water, and juices. Cool slightly. (Otherwise gelatin will congeal. If this does happen, heat just enough to bring back to liquid state.) Just prior to serving time, pour into

*punch bowl; add soda water, frozen raspberries, and sliced bananas.
Stir until raspberries break apart and serve.*

Horn-Tootin' Raspberry Punch A delicious as well as colorful drink for a gala occasion, such as a wedding reception. Yield: 12 punch cups.

> 1 6-oz. can frozen lemonade concentrate, partially thawed
> ½ cup raspberry syrup
> ½ cup grenadine syrup
> ¼ cup superfine sugar
> 3 cups ice water

Pour lemonade concentrate into pitcher. Add sugar, raspberry, and grenadine syrups. Mix thoroughly. Pour ice water into pitcher and stir. Serve at once in glasses filled with crushed or cubed ice.

Rhubarb

Rhubarb Avant-Garde Pretty and delectable drink! Yield: 20 punch cups.

> 1 cup superfine sugar
> 4 cups water
> 2 lbs. rhubarb, cut-up (about 7 cups)
> 1 28-oz. bottle chilled ginger ale

Garnish for ice mold: 12 whole strawberries.

(Prepare ice ring mold according to directions given in Helpful Hints at beginning of this chapter.) Simmer sugar and 1 cup of the water together for 10 minutes. Cool. Put the sliced rhubarb into a pan with the remaining 3 cups of water. Bring to a boil and simmer until tender, about 15 minutes. Strain through a wire sieve, saving juice and reserving pulp. (Sweetened pulp may be served later, as a dessert, with a dab of whipped cream on top.) There

will be about 4½ cups of rhubarb juice. Add the sugar syrup to
rhubarb juice. Chill for 2–3 hours. Pour into punch bowl and add
strawberry ice ring mold. Just prior to serving add the bottle of
ginger ale.

* Gypsy Garnet Punch   Yield: 24 punch cups.

> 2 lbs. rhubarb, cut-up (about 7 cups)
> 2 cups superfine sugar
> 1 qt. water
> 1 pt. strawberries, washed and hulled
> 1 cup orange juice
> 3 tbl. lemon juice
> 1 28-oz. bottle soda water, chilled
> red food coloring

In covered saucepan, slowly heat rhubarb, sugar and water to a
boil. Reduce heat and simmer 15 minutes. Strain through a wire
sieve, saving juice and reserving pulp for dessert treat. Combine
strawberries with ½ cup of the rhubarb syrup in a blender. Blend
on high speed for 1 minute. Stir into remaining rhubarb syrup.
Cool; add orange and lemon juices; chill in refrigerator for 2–3
hours. When ready to serve pour into punch bowl and stir in a few
drops of red food coloring to tint a deep garnet red. At the last
minute, add soda water and serve.

Strawberry

Strawberry Fruit Salad a là Glacé   Be sure to make enough of this
punch as there will certainly be requests for second and third
servings. One of the best punches you have ever tasted. Yield:
56 punch cups.

> 4 cups water
> 4 cups superfine sugar

1¼ cups fresh lemon juice, chilled
2½ cups fresh orange juice, chilled
2 pts. strawberries, sliced
1½ cups crushed pineapple
4 small or 3 large bananas, sliced and quartered
1 cup mixed fruit juice (such as pineapple, raspberry, apricot)
2 28-oz. bottles soda water
4 cups crushed ice

Bring sugar and water to a boil in saucepan. Boil for 5 minutes. Refrigerate for ½ hour. Mix chilled syrup with all fruit juices and cut-up fruits. Just before serving add soda water and crushed ice. This is a rich-flavored punch and the crushed ice will only slightly dilute the flavor.

* Strawberry Fashion Flip   First *in* flavor on the boardwalk. Will be the hit of the show! Yield: 64 punch cups.

8 pts. fresh strawberries
4 cups superfine sugar, or to taste
2 qts. cold ginger ale

Whirl strawberries, a quart at a time in blender until smooth, about 1 minute. Sweeten to taste with approximately 4 cups sugar. Freeze firm in ice cube trays. Just before serving, remove from tray, and put in blender again adding cold ginger ale a little at a time. Blend on low speed for 10 seconds. Serve at once in chilled punch bowl.

Tamarind

Tamarind Tango   For the sweet-toothed adventurous people only. Yield: 8 punch cups.

    4 cups ice water
    1 cup tamarind syrup
    1 pt. tangerine or lime sherbet

Note: You may purchase tamarind syrup at an Oriental food shop. It is citrus-flavored.

Combine ice water, tamarind syrup and sherbet. Stir until sherbet melts slightly. Pour into punch cups and serve.

Watermelon

Swanee River Punch You will enjoy serving this abundant watermelon flavor to your guests. Yield: 24 punch cups.

    6 cups watermelon purée
                or
    2 qts. watermelon chunks
    2 cups fresh lime juice
    2 cups fresh lemon juice
    2 cups fresh orange juice
    1 tsp. salt
    1½ cups sugar
    block of ice

Garnish: lemon, lime and orange slices.

Note: 4 cups of cubed watermelon yields approximately 3 cups of juice.

To prepare watermelon, remove seeds and cut into chunks. In large container, combine watermelon chunks, fruit juices, salt, and sugar. Place half of this mixture in your blender. Cover and turn on high speed for 10 seconds. Take this first portion of blended punch and pour over block of ice in punch bowl. Then place remaining watermelon and juice mixture in blender and blend again.

To complete preparation, add second amount of blended punch to your bowl. For an added colorful touch in the punch, float thin slices of lemon, lime, and orange.

Watermelon Whoopee!   Yield: 12 punch cups.

> 1 medium watermelon (yields 3 qts. juice)
> about 2 cups superfine sugar
> 2 cups ice water

Peel watermelon and cut into walnut-sized chunks. Remove all seeds and press through a sieve or food mill. Add sugar to taste and dilute with ice water. Strain, cool, and serve in well-chilled glasses.

4

HERB TEAS

Helpful Hints

Nineteen Suggested Teas

Gourmet Buds

Helpful Hints

To Brew Herb Teas Use a pottery teapot with its own strainer. Heat your teapot first by pouring boiling water into it. After heating teapot prepare tea by using 1 cup boiling water to 1 teaspoon of fresh or dried herbs *plus* 1 extra teaspoon for the pot. Pour boiling water over leaves and steep 5–10 minutes.

An Exception in Brewing Herb Tea Brewing comfrey leaves is an exception to this process: use 1 cup boiling water to ½ teaspoon comfrey leaves. Cover and steep overnight.

Sweetener for Teas Honey or sugar may be used as a sweetener for teas.

Hot or Iced Tea You may enjoy herb teas hot or iced.

To Brew Seed Teas Crush seeds to emit flavor. Add tea to hot water just before it comes to a boil. Simmer gently for 8–10 minutes. Strain.

Purchasing Teas At specialty food, gourmet, import, and health food stores, you may find these and many other caffeine-free herb teas.

Suggested Teas

A list of teas we have tested and enjoyed!

Alfalfa	Anise
Alfalfa-Mint	Blackberry Leaf

Blueberry Leaf	Fennel
Clover	Lime Tree
Red Clover	Mint
Comfrey	Marjoram
Dill	Papaya-Mint Leaf
Elderberry Leaf	Rose Hips
Eucalyptus	Strawberry Leaf
	Thyme

Gourmet Buds

¼ cup superfine sugar
½ cup rosewater (*or* orange blossom water
or violet water)
4 cups ice water
ice cubes

Note: Rosewater may be made by gently boiling 1 cup water and 5 rose petals for approximately 5 minutes. You may purchase imitation rosewater, orange blossom, or violet flavoring in specialty food stores.

Mix sugar and rosewater. Add 4 cups ice water. Put several ice cubes in each glass and fill glass with rosewater beverage. A truly refreshing drink!

5

MILK BASE

Helpful Hints

Milk-Go-Togethers

Fifty Milk Drinks

Buttermilk Beverages

Helpful Hints

Imitation Buttermilk   To make imitation buttermilk use one cup sweet milk to two teaspoons vinegar or lemon juice. Stir lightly and let stand for ten minutes. *Presto!* Buttermilk for your recipe when you lack the real thing.

Blender Cream   For an economic delicious thick table "cream" use equal parts of dry milk solids and water and add a few drops of yellow food coloring. Mix well with egg beater or blend on low speed for 2–3 seconds *only*.

Blender Skim Milk   Using dry milk solids, follow directions given on the envelope or box. Put water into blender, add the dry milk, cover and mix on low speed for 2–3 seconds *only*. Be careful not to overblend! Serve icy cold.

Blender Skim Shake   Make a delightful shake by combining ⅓ cup dry milk solids with ¾ cup ice water and 1 or 2 tablespoons syrup such as strawberry, maple, raspberry or pineapple. Blend on medium speed for 2–3 seconds *only*.

Milk-Go-Togethers   An especially good way for children or adults alike to enjoy milk more may be to add just a touch of this or that as suggested below!

To one cup of icy cold milk—Stir, blend, or shake:

few drops of food coloring of your choice for a real fiesta of fun
scoop of your favorite flavor ice cream
2–3 tablespoons choice of jam
2–3 tablespoons pancake syrup
2–3 tablespoons thawed fruit juice concentrate

sprinkle of spices such as cinnamon, nutmeg or mace
1 tablespoon molasses plus 2 tablespoons superfine sugar
3–4 tablespoons chocolate syrup
2 teaspoons brown sugar plus 1 teaspoon cinnamon
1 tablespoon superfine sugar plus ¼–½ teaspoon (according to taste)
of any extract listed below:

almond	peppermint
anise	strawberry
mapleine	vanilla
orange	violet

Also, to one cup of icy cold milk, stir, blend, or shake ½ cup chilled and sweetened fruit juice such as listed below:

Apricot	Pineapple
Cherry	Prune
Orange	Raspberry
Peach	Strawberry
	Tangerine

Goat's Milk Improvise For those who enjoy goat's milk, have fun flavoring it with suggestions listed above.

Apple

* **Johnny Appleseed** Serves 2.

2 large eating apples
2 cups milk
¼ cup superfine sugar

Garnish: *touch of cinnamon.*

Core, peel, and cut the apples into small pieces. Pour milk into blender, add apples and sugar. Cover and blend on high speed until frothy, about 30 seconds. Pour into glasses, sprinkle top with cinnamon and serve immediately.

Apple Butter Brew   Serves 1.

> 1 cup cold buttermilk
> 2 tbl. honey
> ½ cup applesauce

Garnish: dash of nutmeg.

Stir all ingredients to mix well. Serve with a dash of nutmeg.

Apricot

* **Drooler**   Serves 3.

> 1½ cups apricot nectar
> 2 cups cold milk
> 1 tbl. lemon juice
> 3 tbl. superfine sugar
> 1 tsp. grenadine syrup

Combine ingredients in blender and blend on high speed for 15 seconds until smooth. A rotary beater or mixer may also be used. Apricot and milk blend is a real palate-pleaser!

* **Bengal Tiger**   Serves 5.

> 2 cups apricot nectar
> 2 cups milk
> 1 pt. vanilla ice cream

Garnish: 5 licorice sticks.

Place all ingredients in blender on high speed for 10 seconds. Remove cover and pour into tall chilled glasses. A real super-duper for you to appreciate! A licorice stick stirrer adds the stripe to your Bengal tiger.

Banana

* **Bona Fide Banana**   A rich banana taste is deliciously apparent in this flavorful sweet drink! Serves 2.

> 2 cups cold milk
> 2 large scoops chocolate ice cream
> 2 ripe bananas

Garnish: whipped cream, grated sweet chocolate.

Combine milk and ice cream in blender. Cover and blend on high speed for 5 seconds. Remove cover and with motor still running, slice in bananas. Blend until smooth. Pour into glasses and top with whipped cream and a sprinkle of grated chocolate.

* **Syncopation Shake**   A great hit with your *rhythm* makers! Serves 6.

> 4 ripe bananas, peeled and sliced
> 1/3 cup orange juice
> 6 tbl. superfine sugar
> touch of salt
> 1/4 tsp. almond extract
> 1 qt. cold milk

Garnish: whipped cream, grated orange rind.

Mash bananas, then beat with remaining ingredients in a mixer or blender until very smooth. (Blender requires 20 seconds on high speed.) Garnish with whipped cream and grated orange rind. A great hit!

* **Chimp Quest**   If you have a menagerie of monkeys—hide this drink as they will surely want to gobble it all up! Serves 1.

1 ripe banana
1 cup cold milk
1 tbl. superfine sugar (optional)

Pour milk into blender; add sliced ripe banana. Cover and blend on medium speed for 10 seconds. Then, increase speed for 10 seconds to complete blending. Serve this good drink in a well-chilled glass. Note: If sugar is included, add when banana is put into blender.

Cantaloupe

* **Bogey Booster**   A boost for before or after golf game. Sure to be a hit with your man! Serves 4.

1 medium-sized ripe cantaloupe
¾ cup cold milk
2 tbl. lemon juice
2 tbl. superfine sugar
1 pt. vanilla ice cream

Peel, seed and slice the cantaloupe into small pieces. Place milk, lemon juice, sugar and cantaloupe in blender. Cover and blend on high speed for 10 seconds. Remove cover and add pint of vanilla ice cream by the scoopfuls. Cover and blend on high speed for 5 seconds. Pour into glasses and enjoy this lip-smackin' drink!

Carbonated Beverages

* **Bon Bon**   Better make two batches—it will go so fast! Serves 2.

2 eggs
½ cup fruit syrup (your choice)

   1 pt. vanilla ice cream
   1 cup ginger ale

Garnish: sprinkle of mace.

Combine chilled ingredients in blender and blend on high speed for 30 seconds. Sprinkle mace on top and serve right away.

Buttermilk Sparkle   Serves 4.

   2 cups buttermilk, chilled
   2 cups ginger ale, chilled

Stir buttermilk and ginger ale together. Pour into iced glasses and serve.

Scooper-Dooper-Spooner   A different twist to a soda. Very cool and refreshing. Serves 1.

   3 scoops orange sherbet
   3 tsp. strawberry jam
   3 scoops vanilla ice cream
   1 7-oz. bottle ginger ale, chilled

Layer in tall glass, one scoop of orange sherbet, 1 teaspoon jam, and 1 scoop vanilla ice cream. Continue until glass is ¾ full. Fill remainder of glass with chilled ginger ale. Serve with straw and long spoon.

Cherry

* Barrel Full of Jelly   Serves 4–6.

   ¼ cup cherry gelatin
   ¼ cup superfine sugar
   ½ cup boiling water
   1 quart cold milk

Place gelatin, sugar, and boiling water in blender. Blend on medium high speed for 20 seconds. Add icy cold milk and blend on high speed another 20 seconds. Chill well in refrigerator. Serve very cold. A good drink that is interestingly different!

Patriotic Cherry Berry Soda   Happy Fourth of July! Serves 1.

> 3–4 tbl. cherry syrup
> ¼ cup cold milk
> ½ cup soda water
> 2 large scoops cherry ice cream

Garnish: whipped cream, chopped maraschino cherries, whole blueberries.

Mix cherry syrup and milk. Add soda water and stir gently. Top with ice cream. Garnish with whipped cream mixed with chopped maraschino cherries and a few blueberries.

Eggnog

Elves' Holly Nog   A scrumptious holiday eggnog. Serves 4.

> 3 eggs, separated
> ½ cup half 'n half
> 2 cups chilled cranberry juice
> ½ tsp. vanilla extract
> 3 tbl. superfine sugar
> few drops red food coloring

Garnish: wreath of live holly.

Place egg yolks in mixing bowl and beat until light and fluffy. Next, beat in half 'n half, cranberry juice, and vanilla until well blended. Just before serving beat egg whites until stiff, but not dry. Add sugar gradually and fold into cranberry mixture. A few drops of red food coloring may be added for color. Serve in punch cups on a tray encircled with a bouquet of holly.

Malt-O-Eggnog   Here is an extra good hot eggnog. (Good cold, too.) Serves 4.

> ¾ cup malted milk powder
> ½ cup boiling water
> 4 eggs, beaten
> 1 qt. milk, heated

Garnish: sprinkle of cinnamon.

Stir malted milk powder and boiling water until smooth. Add eggs and milk. Beat with rotary beater one minute. Pour into cups, sprinkle with cinnamon. If you don't drink it all at once, store remainder in refrigerator and serve cold.

* Scoot Fruit   Serves 2.

> ½ cup pineapple juice
> ½ cup cold milk
> ¼ ripe cantaloupe
> 1 egg

Place all ingredients in blender. Blend on high speed for 20 seconds. Pour into tall glasses. Delicious!

Plushiest Eggnog   Why not serve your husband's boss and his wife this plush eggnog? A sure boss pleaser! Serves 4.

> 6 eggs, separated
> ¾ cup superfine sugar
> 2 tsp. vanilla extract
> 3 cups light cream or whipping cream

Garnish: ground nutmeg.

Beat egg yolks and sugar until light colored and thick. Add vanilla and cream, stir slightly. Now beat the egg whites in a separate bowl until stiff and fold into the eggnog mixture. Pour into glasses. Sprinkle with nutmeg and serve.

* **Cock-a-doodle-doo!**　You will crow with vigor when you taste this. Serves 4.

> 4 cups chilled milk
> 4 eggs
> 4 tbl. superfine sugar
> 1 tsp. vanilla

Garnish: sprinkle of nutmeg.

Place all ingredients in blender and blend on high speed for 15 seconds. Serve in icy cold glasses, sprinkled with nutmeg.

* **Bon Jour Breakfast**　A good-morning taste waker-upper. Serves 1.

> 1 egg
> 1 cup cold milk
> ½ cup chilled fruit (fresh, frozen, or canned)
> ¼ tsp. vanilla

Blend all ingredients on high speed for 30 seconds and serve.

* **Harmony Nog**　This is the ultra-best banana drink ever. Serves 2.

> 1 large ripe banana, peeled and sliced
> 1 egg
> ⅔ cup chilled evaporated milk (6 oz.)
> 1 cup vanilla ice cream
> ½ tsp. vanilla

Garnish: sprinkle of cinnamon.

Blend all ingredients on high speed for 30 seconds. Pour into chilled glasses. Sprinkle with cinnamon. Serve right away.

* Felicitation Nog   For those little tykes who think they don't like milk, serve this to add to their holiday merriment. Serves 5.

> 3 eggs, well beaten
> ¼ cup superfine sugar
> 3 cups chilled milk
> ½ cup orange juice
> 2 tbl. grated orange rind

Blend all ingredients on high speed for 15 seconds and serve. (If rotary beater is used, beat eggs and sugar until light and thick. Add milk, orange juice, and orange rind. Beat until fluffy and serve.)

Vermont Manner   Celebrate Lincoln's Birthday with this refreshment. Serves 4.

> 4 eggs, separated
> 1 cup maple syrup
> 3 cups milk

Using only two egg whites, beat with 4 yolks until lemon colored. Add only ½ cup maple syrup and 3 cups cold milk. Mix well and chill in refrigerator until ready to serve. Make topping just prior to serving.

To prepare topping: Boil remaining ½ cup syrup for 3 minutes. Beat until stiff the remaining 2 egg whites. Pour hot syrup over stiffly-beaten egg whites, and beat until cool. When ready to serve, take chilled milk, syrup, and egg mixture from refrigerator and pour into icy cold glasses. Pour topping over drink for a simple and different touch.

Lemon

Buttercup   Buttermilk lovers—how about serving this little flower?
Serves 4.

> ¾ cup fresh lemon juice
> ½ cup superfine sugar
> 1 qt. buttermilk, chilled
> 2 cups crushed ice

*Mix lemon juice, sugar, and buttermilk. Pour into iced glasses
over ½ cup crushed ice and serve immediately.*

* Mock Lemon Popsicle   Great flavor! Serves 1.

> 4 tbl. frozen lemonade concentrate
> ¾ cup soda water
> 2 scoops vanilla ice cream

Garnish: whipped cream and dehydrated lemon peel.

*Blend all ingredients on high speed for 20 seconds. Garnish with
puff of whipped cream and sprinkle of dehydrated lemon peel.*

Orange

Sunny Start   A thick and delicious drink that is a great start for
any morning. Serves 4.

> 1 can frozen orange juice concentrate (6 oz. size)
> 3 empty juice cans of chilled milk
> 2 tbl. superfine sugar

*Prepare orange juice with milk (instead of water as directed on
cans). Add sugar, beat well, and serve.*

* Milky Way Launch   A glimpse of brightness after a morning of gardening! Serves 2.

> 1 cup orange juice
> ½ cup milk
> 2 slices pineapple (canned)
> thin rind of orange
> 2 scoops vanilla ice cream
> ½ cup crushed ice

Place ingredients in blender on high speed for 10 seconds. Serve pronto!

Papaya

* Frills n' Froth   Exotic flavor! Serves 4.

> 2 large ripe papayas *or* 1 cup papaya nectar
> ⅔ cup superfine sugar
> ¼ cup lime juice
> 3 cups cold milk
> 6 ice cubes

Peel papayas, cut in two, scoop out seeds and mash papaya pulp. Combine all ingredients in blender and blend on high speed for 20 seconds, adding ice cubes one at a time. Serve immediately in well-chilled glasses.

Peach

* Mighty Mite   Serves 1.

> ¼ cup strained canned baby fruit (peaches or your choice
>   of flavor)
> 1 cup cold milk
> sprinkle of cinnamon

Blend all ingredients on high speed for 10 seconds and serve.

* Grand Prix   Really a winner. Serves 2.

   ½ cup chilled peaches
   ½ cup chilled milk
   ⅛ tsp. salt
   ¼ tsp. almond extract
   1 cup vanilla ice cream

 Put all ingredients with the exception of ice cream into blender. Cover and blend on high speed until smooth, about 15 seconds. Add ice cream to this mixture. Cover and blend on low speed for 10 seconds and serve.

Peach Petunia Soda   Serves 1.

   ⅓ cup fresh peaches
   3 tbl. superfine sugar
   ¼ cup cold milk
   ½ cup soda water
   2 scoops peach ice cream

 Garnish: whipped cream, real petunias.

 Mash peaches well; add sugar and cold milk and stir. Slowly add soda water. Stir gently. Top with ice cream. Garnish with a spoon of whipped cream and a real petunia. Extraordinarily good!

Peanut Butter

* Crunchy Peanut Butter Flip   For those ravenous small fry that come in at lunch time. Serves 6.

   4 cups cold milk
   1 pt. vanilla ice cream
   ½ cup peanut butter
   1 pt. chocolate ice cream

 Garnish: whipped cream, crushed peanuts.

Put milk, vanilla ice cream, and peanut butter into blender. Cover and blend on high speed for 30 seconds. Pour into glasses and top with two scoops of chocolate ice cream. Top with puff of whipped cream mixed with crushed peanuts. Yummy!

* Peanut Butter Triplet   A real hit with the peanut butter crowd. Serves 3.

> ½ cup plus 1 tbl. peanut butter
> 3 tbl. honey
> 3 cups cold milk

Blend peanut butter and honey until well mixed. Slowly add 3 cups cold milk to blender with motor on low speed for 15 seconds. Serve.

Note: A rotary beater may be used instead. Beat all ingredients well and serve.

Persimmon

* Apogee   This is the apex of a taste treat. Serves 1.

> 1 cup cold milk
> ¾ cup persimmon, peeled and sliced
> ¼ cup powdered milk
> 1 tbl. superfine sugar
> 1 tsp. vanilla extract
> 1 egg

Blend all ingredients on high speed for 15 seconds until smooth. Serve immediately in chilled glasses.

Note: This recipe may be used as a great variation recipe by substituting apricots, bananas, peaches, pineapple, or strawberries for the persimmons.

Pineapple

Poolside Sip   Serves 4.

>3 cups cold milk
>2 cups pineapple juice, chilled
>¾ cup light cream
>¼ cup superfine sugar
>⅛ cup lemon juice
>6 drops peppermint extract

Garnish: pineapple spears, sprigs of mint.

Combine all ingredients and beat with rotary beater until foamy. Pour into glasses. Serve with straws. Garnish with pineapple spear and a sprig of mint.

Little Miss Muffet's Curds and Pineapple   Serves 1.

>1 cup ice cold buttermilk
>½ cup pineapple juice

Whip together buttermilk and pineapple juice. Serve immediately to all who enjoy buttermilk.

Plum

* Little Jack Horner's Plum-Good   Serves 2.

>1½ cups plums fresh or canned
>2 cups milk
>1 pt. vanilla ice cream

Garnish: whipped cream, purple grapes.

If fresh plums are used, add ¼ cup superfine sugar to them after removing pits and peeling. Blend all ingredients on high speed for 15 seconds. Pour into glasses and top with spoon of whipped cream and a few purple grapes.

* Plum Peachy   Serves 4.

> 1 cup sliced peaches, fresh or canned
> 1 cup red plums
> ¼ cup corn syrup
> 3 cups cold milk
> 1 tray ice cubes (16)

Combine all ingredients except ice cubes in blender. Turn on high speed for 10 seconds. Then turn to low speed, adding ice cubes one at a time until all are finely crushed. Pour into glasses and serve right away.

Prune

Pioneer Prune   Serves 2.

> 1 4-oz. can chilled prune juice
> ⅓ cup chilled orange juice
> 1 cup cold milk
> touch of salt
> 1 tsp. fresh lemon juice
> 1 or 2 tbl. superfine sugar
> 1 large scoop vanilla ice cream

Garnish: *twists of orange slices.*

Pour prune juice, orange juice, and milk into a large bowl. Add salt, lemon juice, sugar, and ice cream. With rotary beater blend thoroughly. Top each glass with a twist of orange slice.

Pumpkin

* **Goblin's Gulp**   Cut out and paste black paper cats on glasses. This drink has a beautiful color and is a luscious way to enjoy pumpkin! Great for those "trick or treaters" at your house. Serves 2.

>   2 eggs
>   ¼ cup superfine sugar
>   1 cup canned pumpkin
>   2 cups cold milk
>   4 scoops vanilla ice cream
>   sprinkle of nutmeg
>   touch of cinnamon

Place all ingredients in blender container. Turn speed on low to begin blending. Increase to medium for 10 seconds, then to high speed for 10 seconds to complete blending. Pour into tall, chilled glasses.

Raspberry

* **Crimson Supreme**   The raspberry flavor is a delight in this frothy and delectable drink. Serves 4.

>   1 10-oz. package frozen raspberries, partially thawed
>   3 cups cold milk
>   1 tbl. superfine sugar
>   1 tbl. lemon juice
>   touch of salt

Blend all ingredients on high speed for 10 seconds. Pour into chilled glasses. Serve.

* Raspberry Blush   Serves 2.

>   1 cup cold milk
>   2 large scoops raspberry sherbet

Combine cold milk and sherbet in blender. Cover and blend on high speed for 15 seconds. Really luscious!

* Berry, Berry Good   Serves 4.

>   1 10-oz. package frozen raspberries, partially thawed
>   3 cups cold milk
>   ¼ tsp. almond extract
>   1 pt. strawberry ice cream

Put berries, milk, and almond into blender. Cover and blend on high speed for 30 seconds until smooth. Add half the ice cream and blend on low speed for 10 seconds. Pour into glasses and top each glass with a scoop of remaining ice cream and serve.

Spice

* Candy Boat Splash   When it's party time for children try this welcome treat. Serves 4.

>   ¼ cup honey
>   3 cups cold milk
>   1 tsp. ground cinnamon
>   ¼ tsp. each ginger and nutmeg
>   1 pt. peach ice cream
>   few drops food coloring (your choice color)

Garnish: 12 sliced gumdrops, 4 little paper flags.

Begin by putting honey, milk, and spices into blender. Cover and turn on low speed for 30 seconds. Pour into tall glasses and top with a huge scoop of ice cream. Spoon topping of sliced gumdrops on ice cream. Insert flag and serve.

Snow Cream   Have you ever watched the joy and exuberance of children eating fresh snow? Now you can offer a special snow drink for all and join in the fun of making it. Serves 5.

>   1 gal. new fallen snow (scoop carefully so as not to get dirt)
>   1 qt. milk, chilled
>   3 tbl. vanilla
>   2 cups superfine sugar

Scoop new fallen snow into very large container. Add milk, sugar and vanilla, stirring gently to mix well. Pour into tall glasses and serve with long-handled spoons and straws.

Strawberry

* **Strawberry Blonde**   This luscious milkshake can be a crowning glory to a simple lunch on a torrid day. Serves 2.

>   1 cup cold milk
>   1 cup orange juice, chilled
>   1 10-oz. package frozen strawberries, partially thawed
>   2 scoops vanilla ice cream

Garnish: whipped cream (colored pink with a drop or two of red food coloring).

Blend all ingredients on high speed for 20 seconds, until smooth. Serve with puff of pink whipped cream.

Snowy Strawberry Peak   Scrumptious drink! The peak of perfection. Serves 8.

1 10-oz. package sliced frozen strawberries
   or
1 pt. fresh sweetened sliced strawberries
4 cups cold milk
1 pt. strawberry ice cream
2 tsp. grated lemon peel (available in dehydrated form)
1 28-oz. bottle soda water

Garnish: *whipped cream, 8 fresh strawberries with hulls on.*

Thaw frozen strawberries partially. If fresh strawberries are in season, you may slice, sweeten, and crush them. In chilled bowl, place berries, milk, lemon peel, and ice cream. Beat with electric mixer on high speed for one minute. Pour evenly into tall, chilled glasses filling to the top with soda water. Top with whipped cream and a fresh strawberry in season. Serve at once.

* **Pink Sailing**   Serves 1.

1 cup cold milk
3 tsp. strawberry preserves
1 scoop vanilla ice cream

Beat all ingredients together using blender or mixer, to consistency you prefer. (Blend about 15 seconds on high speed. Beat about 3 minutes with mixer.)

Yoghurt

* **Yoghurt Yowl**   Yoghurt lovers will howl over this yummy yoghurt drink. Serves 3.

1 cup yoghurt (plain)
¼ tsp. salt
dash of pepper

2 cups ice water
4 thin strips lemon peel
dash Tabasco
½ teaspoon fresh chopped mint

Blend all ingredients on high speed for 15 seconds. Serve immediately in frosted glasses. (Dip plastic glasses in water, put in freezer for 10–15 minutes.)

* **Gay Blade**   An icy cold and flavorful drink. Serves 2.

½ cup yoghurt
1 cup pineapple, crushed
½ cup strawberries
½ cup papaya juice

Blend all ingredients on medium speed for 10 seconds. Increase to high speed for another 10 seconds. Serve at once.

* **Taste Teaser**   A delightful way to start the day. Serves 1.

1 envelope instant powdered vanilla breakfast drink
1 cup milk, chilled
¼ cup yoghurt (your favorite flavor)

Pour milk, breakfast drink, and yoghurt into blender. Blend on medium speed for 10 seconds, then on high speed for an additional 10 seconds.

6

VEGETABLE BASE

Helpful Hints

Eighteen Vegetable Drinks

Special Hot Drinks

Steaming Sips
or Frigid Plunges

Helpful Hints

Blending Vegetables   Always add liquid to blender before chopped vegetables. You will prolong the life of your blender.

Hint for Blender Cover   Just a reminder! When recipe calls for added ingredients: while motor is running, remove feeder cap and add a little at a time. If your blender has no feeder cap, turn motor off, add ingredients and turn motor on again to continue blending.

Asparagus

* **Asparagus Pepper-Upper**   Serves 4.

> 1   10½-oz. can cream of asparagus soup
> 1¼   soup cans of cold milk
> ¾   tsp. celery salt
> ½   tsp. ground pepper
> ¼   cup lemon juice

Garnish: sprinkle paprika.

Put all ingredients into blender and blend on high speed for 1 minute. Pour into glasses and sprinkle with paprika. May be served hot also for a luscious appetizer.

Carrot

* **Gourmets' Caper**   Serves 4.

> 1   medium carrot, cut in 6 pieces
> 1   can condensed cream of chicken soup

110

1 cup canned condensed chicken consommé
½ tsp. celery salt
½ tsp. onion salt

Garnish: ½ cup nondairy whipped topping, dash of paprika.

Blend all ingredients except whipped topping until smooth—about 1 minute on high speed. Remove to saucepan and heat. Serve hot. Top each serving with a dollop of whipped topping and a dash of paprika. This makes a delicious lunch served with crackers and cheese.

Rabbit Raid   Serves 2.

2 cups carrot juice
2 cups grapefruit juice
¼ cup superfine sugar, if desired

Garnish: 2 slices of carrot, for stirrers.

Mix juices and chill thoroughly. Serve with a carrot stirrer.

Bottoms Up   Serves 2.

½ cup carrot juice
1½ cups tomato juice
dash Worcestershire sauce

Mix chilled juices well and serve.

Celery

Celery Crisp   So good! Serves 4.

4 cups tomato juice, chilled
1 cup celery juice, chilled
celery seed

Garnish: 4 slices of celery, 4 olives, green or black.

Mix juices well; pour into chilled glasses; sprinkle with celery seed. Add stirrers of celery stick studded with an olive on top and serve.

Clam

* Old-Fashioned Clam Shake A truly delightful clam drink! Serves 4.

> ¼ cup catsup
> ½ tsp. horseradish
> 1 medium onion, thinly sliced
> 1 stalk celery, cut in 1 in. pieces
> 2 cups clam juice

Place all ingredients, except clam juice, in blender. Turn blender on high speed until onion and celery are liquefied. With blender running uncover small opening in lid and gradually add the clam juice. Continue blending for 10 seconds. Serve icy cold in mugs.

* Clamdigger's Cup   Serves 6.

> 4 cups tomato juice
> 2 cups clam juice
> ¼ cup lemon juice
> dash of Worcestershire sauce
> ⅛ tsp. salt
> ⅛ tsp. pepper

Garnish: 6 lemon slices, cut ¼ in. thick.

Chill juices thoroughly. Just before serving, place all ingredients in blender and whirl on high speed for 10–15 seconds. Serve in well-iced cups and garnish with lemon slices.

Cucumber

* Terrestrial Delight   A beautiful green color with interesting different flavor that is sure to please the taste. Serves 2.

>   1 cup unsweetened pineapple juice, chilled
>   1 cup cucumber, seeded and peeled
>   2 sprigs of watercress
>   ½ cup finely crushed ice

Garnish: sprigs of watercress.

Place juice, cucumber, watercress, and ice in blender. Cover and turn on low speed for 5 seconds. Increase speed to medium high for 15 seconds. Then increase to high for 20 seconds. Will be thick and frothy—similar to consistency of a milkshake. Garnish with sprigs of watercress.

* Coo-Coo Cucumber   Serves 6.

>   1½ cups cucumber, seeded, peeled and chopped
>   1 qt. buttermilk
>   1 tbl. finely chopped green onions
>   1 tsp. salt
>   ¼ cup finely chopped parsley
>   1 tsp. monosodium glutamate
>   dash of pepper

Garnish: dash of paprika, cucumber slices.

Blend all ingredients on low speed for one minute. Chill thoroughly 3–4 hours. Just before serving, mix and pour into chilled glasses. Garnish with slices of cucumber and a dash of paprika.

Sauerkraut

Sauerbraten Flip   Serves 6.

> 6 cups tomato juice, chilled
> 2 cups sauerkraut juice, chilled
> 1 tsp. horseradish
> 1 tbl. superfine sugar

Mix all ingredients well. Serve this spicy drink with a sauerbraten dinner.

Peppy Prelude   A good appetizer! It's mouth puckerin' good. Serves 6.

> 3 cups sauerkraut juice
> 1 cup tomato juice
> 1 tsp. lemon juice
> ⅛ tsp. paprika
> ½ tsp. horseradish, optional

Put all ingredients in shaker. Shake vigorously for 3–5 minutes. Chill thoroughly. Must be very cold when served.

Tomato

Hot Tomato Squeeze   Serves 5.
> 1 28-oz. can tomatoes
> 1 18-oz. can tomato juice
> ½ onion
> 1 clove garlic
> 1 bay leaf

    3 whole peppercorns
    touch of salt
    sprinkle of celery salt
    ¼ tsp. Worcestershire sauce

Garnish: ½ cup nondairy whipped topping mixed with 1 tbl. horseradish.

Place canned tomatoes in blender. Blend to puree. Pour into saucepan and add can of tomato juice, onion, garlic, bay leaf, and peppercorns. Heat to gentle boil. Then, simmer for 30 minutes. Strain and season with next three ingredients. Serve bubbling hot in mugs or icy cold with a garnish of whipped topping mixed with horseradish.

* Tossed Appeal   Great as replacement for tossed salad at hearty meal. Serves 4.

    2 cups tomato juice
    1 cucumber, peeled, seeded, chopped
    1 tbl. vinegar
    ½ tsp. salt
    ⅛ tsp. paprika
    ¼ tsp. basil
    1 cup crushed ice

Place all ingredients in blender on high speed for 20 seconds or until cucumber is liquefied. Serve icy cold.

* Bravo—Orange and Tomato   A wonderful flavor that will prove superb for all. Serves 4.

    1½ cups tomato juice
    1 cup orange juice
    1 tsp. sugar
    1 tbl. lemon juice

> ½ tsp. salt
> ½ cup crushed ice

Garnish: 4 lemon wedges.

Combine all ingredients in blender or shaker until well mixed. Serve immediately with a garnish of lemon wedge.

Tomato Bouquet　Serves 4.

> 1 14-oz. can tomato juice
> 1 tsp. dried onion flakes
> 1 tsp. celery seed
> ¼ tsp. Worcestershire sauce
> ½ tsp. superfine sugar
> ½ tsp. salt
> 2-in. stick of cinnamon
> ½ tsp. horseradish

Garnish: Vegetable kababs made with chunks of green pepper, cocktail onions, olives, cauliflowerette, cucumber slice, and radish slice on a toothpick!

Combine ingredients. Chill 2 hours. Strain and serve over cracked ice with a garnish of vegetable kabab. This drink is delicious served hot in mugs too!

Love Apple and Pineapple A.M.　A great way to enjoy two juices in one glass! Serves 4.

> 1 cup pineapple juice, chilled
> 1 cup tomato juice, chilled
> sprinkle of salt

Combine all ingredients in shaker. Shake vigorously for about 1 minute. Pour into juice glasses and serve icy cold for a tasty breakfast drink.

Blush Tomato Brunch   Serve hot on a cool rainy day in a cozy, warm home with a crackling fire in the fireplace. As a cool treat, you may enjoy serving icy cold for a hot summer day brunch. Either way it is a great accompaniment. Serves 5.

> 4 cups tomato juice
> 1 cup canned beef consomme
> touch of garlic powder
> sprinkle of parsley flakes
> ¼ tsp. marjoram
> ¼ tsp. thyme

Simply heat ingredients until steaming hot and serve. (For serving cold: Combine ingredients and chill in refrigerator until ready to serve.)

Veteran's Day Rooty-Tooty   Serves 6.

> 1 46-oz. can tomato juice
> 6 tbl. brown sugar
> 6 whole cloves
> 4-in. stick of cinnamon
> 6 slices of lemon, ¼ in. thick

Garnish: 6 sticks of cinnamon.

Combine all ingredients in saucepan. Bring to a boil and simmer for 5 minutes. Strain. Serve piping hot in mugs with a small piece of stick cinnamon as a garnish.

Holiday Beverages' Calendar

Beverage Guide

for All Occasions

Beach Parties

Brunches

Children's Parties

Wedding Receptions

Index

Additional recipes are listed in the Holiday Beverages' Calendar on page 119 and in the Beverage Guide for All Occasions, page 121.